The End of Office Politics as Usual

The End of Office Politics as Usual

A Complete Strategy for
Creating a More Productive and
Profitable Organization

Lawrence B. MacGregor Serven

AMACOM

American Management Association

New York • Atlanta • Brussels • Buenos Aires • Chicago • London • Mexico City
San Francisco • Shanghai • Tokyo • Toronto • Washington, D.C.

Special discounts on bulk quantities of AMACOM books are available to corporations, professional associations, and other organizations. For details, contact Special Sales Department, AMACOM, a division of American Management Association, 1601 Broadway, New York, NY 10019.
Tel.: 212-903-8316. Fax: 212-903-8083.
Web site: www.amacombooks.org.

This publication is designed to provide accurate and authoritative information in regard to the subject matter covered. It is sold with the understanding that the publisher is not engaged in rendering legal, accounting, or other professional service. If legal advice or other expert assistance is required, the services of a competent professional person should be sought.

Library of Congress Cataloging-in-Publication Data

Serven, Lawrence B. MacGregor.
    The end of office politics as usual : a complete strategy for creating a more productive and profitable organization / Lawrence B. MacGregor Serven.
        p.   cm.
    Includes bibliographical references and index.
    ISBN 0-8144-0664-5
    1. Office politics.   2. Organizational change.   I. Title.

HF5386.5 .S48 2001
650.1'3—dc21   2001034088

Printing number

10   9   8   7   6   5   4   3   2   1

DEDICATION

*One day when I was in the middle of researching this book
and feeling overwhelmed, Susan, my wife,
told me what had happened to her that same day. She had been
building from scratch a dollhouse for our
then-three-year-old daughter, Emily. It was painstaking work,
and Susan encountered one challenge after another. She
became so frustrated that she wanted to forget the whole
thing. Ever been there? Emily looked at her and said,
"But, Mommy, that's your dream." Indeed, it was.*

*You're looking at my dream.
Thank you, Susan and Emily,
for not letting me ever forget it.*

*The trouble with the rat race is that even
if you win, you're still a rat.*
— Lily Tomlin

*The fault, dear Brutus, is not in our stars,
But in ourselves.*
— William Shakespeare

We have met the enemy, and he is us.
— Walt Kelly's Pogo

Contents

Prologue
Taking Aim at Building Nine

Men build too many walls and not enough bridges.
—SIR ISAAC NEWTON

Microsoft is a company people love to hate. It's like a high school football team from an affluent town that keeps winning the divisional conference year after year. Sure, its players are good, but we can't wait until they fall flat on their keisters.

Yet it's worth suspending our animosity long enough to examine what's at the root of Microsoft's success and learn from it. Microsoft is, after all, among the most successful companies of our time, and its stockholders have been richly rewarded for its performance. Just think, if you had scraped together $10,000 in 1990 and bought Microsoft stock, you'd be a multimillionaire today. Microsoft has triumphed in spite of being in an industry that changes constantly, of being subject to Wall Street's roller-coaster ride, and of facing many challenges in antitrust litigation.

What's been the wellspring of Microsoft's success? In plain language, most companies do battle with two sets of enemies—the enemy outside and the enemy inside. Microsoft owes much of its success to having narrowed its list of enemies to those outside the company. It sounds simple enough. But how did Microsoft do it? If you spend enough time at the company, somebody's bound to tell you the following story. It's become part of the rich company lore and helps explain Microsoft's unrivaled success.

A few years ago two marketing groups at Microsoft were battling each other, just as marketing groups in companies so often do. Each group tried to position itself for greater decision-making authority and a larger budget than the other. Each group perceived itself as a stand-alone squad, not as part of one unified Microsoft team. They argued over everything—from spending, to sharing customer names, to communications plans and launch dates, to you name it. Factions popped up like weeds, and frustration swelled. People began to make decisions based not on what was best for the business, but on what was best for their fiefdoms. In short, office politics ran rampant, and the Microsoft team splintered. But in the midst of all this mayhem, someone saw the truth and had the courage to say, "Our competition is WordPerfect, Novell, and Lotus, not Building Nine."

This simple statement struck everybody as direct and profound. It spread quickly across the Microsoft campus and is repeated to this day whenever turf battles and other forms of office politics begin to threaten good decision making.

Good slogan, you might be thinking, *but how does it work in practice? How does this idea really affect the decisions people make every day?*

To understand, use your imagination and place yourself in the following scene. Suppose that you were the product manager for Microsoft Office when it was first introduced. As a product manager, you would live for a moment like this one. You've just hit the big time with a national product rollout!

Being a typical product manager then, you certainly intend to make the most of this windfall. The objective, from your career perspective, is to build your own marketing empire.

First of all, you'll need your own national advertising and promotional campaign. Everyone knows you're judged by the size of your budget, and you should be able to garner a pretty fat one if you play your cards right. Who knows? You might even be able to hire a dedicated sales force. Even if it's just a small one, a dedicated sales force is a sure sign that your empire is growing and you're someone to be reckoned with.

Now comes the irritating part. Windows is launching a new version, too. That marketing group thinks it would be a good idea to launch the two programs together. Its people talk about how much money a combined launch will save the company and how it will provide one unified message to the customer about the Microsoft "family" of products. They say it's in the best interest of the company as a whole.

What planet are these guys from? you wonder. *They're a separate group! They really need to grow up.*

So you claim that your audiences are different, insist you really need to establish a separate message, tell them there's an inherent incompatibility of the two different marketing approaches, and so on. "But," you carefully add so nobody can accuse you later of not being a team player, "if you want to do a couple of selected cross-promotion programs, just pull together a plan and a budget. We'll take a look at it."

Thus, you have squandered a big opportunity for the company to save money and simultaneously improve product promotion and sales just because you think it will diminish your budding empire. Although you wouldn't admit it to anyone, you know you're playing office politics, in this case engaging in a turf battle to establish your own empire. To you, you are just acting in your own self-interest. To the company though, you've just become the "enemy within."

Even though your employer certainly doesn't condone political behavior, no one is stopping you, either. It's just the way it is.

But hold on here. Stop the presses. This business isn't an average company—it's Microsoft. Forget about the speculative and the hypothetical; let me tell you what actually did happen.

The product managers for Microsoft Office and Microsoft Windows decided to launch the products together rather than run two separate and potentially competing marketing programs. The product manager for Microsoft Office even designed his product's box with the same blue-and-white clouds that appeared on the new Windows program box. Microsoft Office appeared in the new Windows launch events rather than staging its own, and it actually marketed its program's compatibility with the new Windows version.

The outcome of this joint venture was that Microsoft Office made its sales projections while spending considerably less on marketing than it would have with a separate plan. The two groups were also able to present a single, unified message to Microsoft customers, bolstering sales for all

Microsoft products. In short, separate interests in Microsoft came together to do what was best for the company as a whole.

Who benefited from this decision? First, the company and its shareholders benefited from running a more effective marketing campaign for less money. That's what business is all about. Its success also reinforced the value of making the best business decision for the company rather than for any one department. At an individual level, the product managers benefited, also, because their expertise as marketing professionals grew by running a strategically driven campaign. There's a good reason why Microsoft employees are so aggressively sought after by recruiters.

"Good story," you say. "I see the point. But does that one story explain all of the company's incredible growth in sales and profits?"

Of course not. The story, however, illustrates this point: A passion for doing what's best for the business as a whole rather than battling an enemy within was and is behind the thousands of decisions people make in the Microsoft enterprise every day.

This premise does not overlook the fact that Microsoft has its share of problems or that the company will have to work hard to continue to dominate the marketplace given emerging technologies and an ever growing warren of competitors. But what we can say is this: Success is built one decision at a time, and in Microsoft, those decisions are not driven by internal politics, but by the best interests of the company and its stockholders. This basic position is what forms the absolute nucleus of their success.

Take note that in the example of the product manager at Microsoft nothing was "reengineered," "downsized," or "continually improved." Nobody needed to be "empowered" to become "customer intimate," and no one went to work in a "quality circle." Stop and think for a moment. Would any of these popular initiatives or programs have changed the product manager's approach? Absolutely not, and knowing that is why you cringe every time such an initiative is announced at your company. What you know instinctively is that people will continue to act in their own self-interests, and as long as those self-interests are at odds with those of the organization, performance will continue to suffer no matter what else happens.

In the average company, for instance, a product manager's self-interest will be served by increasing the size of her budget, by garnering a dedicated sales force, and by a host of other factors that have little to do with actually making money. At Microsoft, self-interest is served by making the best possible business decision, the one that will create the most value and build the most wealth for the whole organization.

The question, then, is, How can you make that happen? How can you diminish political behavior and instead focus everyone on doing the right thing, on making the right decisions for the organization as a whole?

If that question intrigues you, perhaps it is because you have some personal experience, as many of us have, with office politics. Perhaps you have recently entered or reentered the workplace. You joined your company with an enthusiasm that began to drain away after your first "reality shock," such as the first time you saw good money being thrown after bad simply because an important person wanted a pet project funded.

Perhaps you have been in the workforce for quite awhile, have seen a succession of bad decisions made for all the wrong reasons, and wondered, *Why do we allow this nonsense to keep happening?*

Perhaps you are a leader in an organization and have seen so much rivalry between different factions that you wonder whether you'll ever accomplish anything.

Perhaps you are a consultant who has seen repeatedly the powerful resistance inside a company to implementing "the right answer," no matter how good that answer might be.

What do all of you have in common? You share a feeling deep down that there simply has to be a better way of doing business. There is. The best companies have already discovered it.

In the following pages you'll learn about these companies and how they overcome the enemy within. You'll also see how other companies have gotten into trouble by ignoring the problem. Along the way you will also discover something important: You are neither crazy nor naïve to want a better workplace, one in which people who play by the rules win, where people are rewarded based on merit, and where people know the only enemy they should be fighting is *outside* the company. You are certainly not alone in your desire. Your goal is not only achievable, but also highly desirable for your stockholders and employees alike.

So read on, and have courage that your instinct has been right all along.

The End of Office
Politics as Usual

Introduction
The Enemy Within

Discontent is the first necessity of progress.
—THOMAS EDISON

I n his book *A Study of History*, Arnold Toynbee traced the rise and fall of twenty-one civilizations. He discovered at the end of his monumental effort that declines in civilizations came from an unexpected source. Civilizations did not succumb to barbarian attacks or natural disasters.

The enemy came from within.

Toynbee argues these civilizations failed because of internal divisiveness, wrangling, and obstinacy, all of which left their societies weakened and acutely vulnerable. While Rome survived one thousand years of near ceaseless battles, its government could not survive its own corruption. It fell prey to the enemy within.

Are there business lessons about office politics to be learned here? You bet there are, and in this book we'll cover those lessons. First, though, to put it all in proper perspective, we need to assess the strength of our business communities today. Here's where we stand:

- A reader survey in *CFO Magazine* in July 1988 revealed that two-thirds of respondents feel their companies' plans are driven more by politics than by strategy.

1

• According to a study by the *Wall Street Journal,* more than one-third of those people surveyed would willingly move to another state for a job that would give them peace of mind. They would forgo money or status just for less stress.

• Using eleven different criteria, a Gallup Poll asked people about their current job satisfaction. Fewer than half the people said they experienced satisfaction from *any* item on the poll's list.

• A study conducted by the Center for Workforce Development at Rutgers University found that 88 percent of 6,000 workers surveyed experience workplace stress and are concerned about it.[1]

This report card isn't good. What's going on here? We could summarize the sentiments expressed in the above studies with just one word—disappointment. But with what exactly are workers disappointed?

The Search for a Corporate Viagra

People in the workplace are disappointed with the myriad initiatives and programs that they've encountered in management's never ending quest for something, anything, to improve the company's performance. Rather than face the realities revealed in this book, management often desperately grabs hold of the promise of a quick fix. Management searches for a sort of corporate Viagra, something that will enhance performance in one easy-to-take dose.

When one program doesn't work, management tries another one and quickly follows up with yet another. You probably know them all: reengineering, downsizing, customer intimacy, and continuous improvement. Some of these programs turn out to be simply irrelevant, but others actually undermine the possibility of real change by engendering widespread cynicism and skepticism among the workers.

The pivotal question, then, is, Why do these efforts fail? They fail because they are based on a fundamentally flawed assumption.

Nearly every business book, improvement process, or consulting program presupposes one fundamental factor: They all assume that everyone in an organization is working in the company's best interests. They don't account for masterminding, or deceit, in the workplace or for a lack of cooperation between departments or people. They believe that the workers only need knowledge—the knowledge of a better way to do their jobs.

But is that assumption true for your organization? Of course not. Given the presence of office politics, or what I call "the enemy within," any attempts to implement improvement efforts end in frustration, misgivings, and increased cynicism (not to mention money forfeited on consulting fees).

No wonder a recent survey documented that 83 percent of all improvement efforts fail to live up to their claims.[2] Companies have spent hundreds of millions of dollars in the past few years on improvement efforts that never paid off. Thus, companies must address the enemy within if any of their other initiatives stand a chance of being successful.

The Quality of Work Life

What other factors explain workers' disappointment with their work lives? Is it that the world is growing more competitive every year and that the already hectic pace of change itself is accelerating rapidly? Is it that people are working longer and harder as a result? That line of reasoning might sound logical enough, but it's way off track.

Workers' disappointment is not about the number of hours they work, the intensity of their deadlines, or the amount of effort they expend on the job. Their dissatisfaction stems from the poor quality of their work lives.

This conclusion is borne out by an eight-year study of executives at Illinois Bell after AT&T's divestiture.[3] Researchers Salvatore Maddi and Suzanne Kobasa Ouellette studied executives who worked under stressful circumstances. Maddi and Ouellette found that the stress took a toll on many of the study's participants, as evidenced by their suffering from a whole host of physical ailments. A small group among the executives, however, showed no signs of stress. People in this latter group had three things in common:

JA prob?

Sense of control. They felt that they had a strong influence or authority over the outcomes and results for which they were held accountable.

Sense of challenge. They felt that the monumental task of reconfiguring Illinois Bell, and their specific role in it, was a worthwhile personal challenge.

Sense of shared commitment. They felt a strong bond and even emotional ties to the organization and to the goals and challenges it faced.

These crucial factors positively affected the quality of the executives' work lives.

What People Really Want

Having looked at some of the sources of frustration and dissatisfaction in the workplace, what do people really want out of their work lives anyway?

One of the nation's largest cable broadcasters had been experiencing what they told my company were "people problems." In short, morale was at an all-time low, there was virtually no cooperation between different groups and units, and the company had missed nearly every one of its performance targets for the previous five quarters.

"These people are driven by incentives," the president of the company told us, "but we've done all we can do with bonus payouts, our benefits package—you name it. We can't continue to justify paying people the way we are now," he said, as he stabbed his desk with his finger, "while our performance continues to sink."

As a first step in helping this company, we conducted a survey to determine what people wanted out of their work environment and how their current situation stacked up against that. We discovered that the president's basic assumption was incorrect. His people expressed less concern about money than they did about the quality of their work lives.

Above all, his employees wanted to be able trust their leadership and each other. They wanted straight talk and an open sharing of information and opinions. They wanted a cooperative and supportive work environment. They also valued a sense of community, honesty, and fair play. They valued consistent and ethical treatment for all employees. They did not want secrets, backbiting, hidden agendas, or masterminding. Money, as it turned out, was nowhere near the central factor in job satisfaction that the president thought it was.

What people want in their work lives is not that complicated or elaborate. It boils down to a desire to feel part of something larger than themselves. They want a work environment where the only enemy to be found is *outside* the walls of the company. They want to be a part of a workplace where everybody knows the rules, where the people who play by them win, where people are rewarded based on merit, and where results matter more than personalities. In the absence of these things, the enemy begins to grow within the company.

The Enemy Within (a.k.a. Office Politics)

In the absolute broadest terms, we experience the enemy within when we don't feel safe. When we discover that people who play by the rules don't win after all and that people are rewarded for something other than merit, we find ourselves engaged in office politics.

We know we are better than this, and we *are* better than this. Battling the enemy within has nothing at all to do with hard work; it is simply a waste of time and talent. Many "new economy" companies use the acronym "WOMBAT"—or waste of money, brains, and time—to describe office politics.

Crazy Old Aunt Natalie, *or* Why This Book Was Written

My first book, *Value Planning: The New Approach to Building Value Every Day*, explains how shareholder value (the price of a share of common stock multiplied by all the outstanding shares) ultimately depends on the decisions workers make on the front lines every day.[4] Thus, the better those daily decisions are, the better the company's performance, the greater the investors' confidence in the company and its management, and the higher the stock's price. Although it's not complicated, it certainly isn't easy.

The trick is to build a management system to align all the interests of the company's employees behind clear and focused organizational goals and priorities, creating, in a sense, one unified team across the enterprise that is focused on winning. Many companies, however, lack the mechanisms, systems, and structure to make it happen. *Value Planning* sought to change that by providing a hands-on blueprint.

There was one important but admittedly unintended consequence of this work. In many cases companies not only created explosive shareholder value, the people in those companies also found their work lives dramatically transformed. Gone in these instances was "politics as usual," or the backbiting and masterminding that had previously characterized their workplaces.

In its place workers found an organization dedicated to achieving clear goals, and to pulling together as a single cohesive team to make them a reality for both personal and organizational payoffs. Even though people were sometimes working harder, they felt inspired and trusted each other more. They actually felt energized by coming to work every day and rewarded in ways they couldn't even conceive of before.

Frankly, I was surprised and intrigued. What exactly was it that drove an organization once characterized by political infighting to become a unified team, one characterized by high achievement, trust, and personal satisfaction? What was the engine of this workplace transformation? And why didn't it work in all cases? Could the necessary prerequisites, the ones that success absolutely hinged upon, be isolated? Finally, what body of work could be used and built upon to make the chance of transformation even greater and the results even stronger?

One inescapable conclusion I reached is that the way in which a company handles office politics, known by many different names and forms, is a crucial determinant in its ability to improve its performance. I chose therefore to dedicate my firm's key resources to investigating this phenomenon and to study professionally what had been largely ignored as a serious business issue.

In many ways, office politics have been treated like your crazy old aunt, Natalie, living in the attic. You know she's there, but what can you really do about her anyway? "What noise? Oh, that noise—mice in the attic. We just can't get rid of 'em."

To be honest, the professional community hasn't been much help with this topic. They're just as embarrassed and uncomfortable talking about crazy old Natalie as you are. They'd rather talk to you about establishing synergies, reducing cycle times, and building customer intimacy and quality circles. They can discuss those issues openly and seem more dignified and professional. The only problem is that none of their proposed changes—be it reengineering or balanced scorecards—can be implemented effectively with crazy Aunt Natalie still in the attic. People just can't think straight with all that distracting noise, not to mention all the energy that's expended pretending that it's not a problem while still having to work around it.

To be fair, people have written about office politics before, but more often than not they have added to the problem and not worked to reform it. A quick search on Amazon.com shows at least two dozen books that allegedly describe all the nasty tricks and insider secrets you'll ever need to know to get ahead in a political organization. To promote themselves, these new books have tried to outdo their predecessors on the down and dirty "guerilla tactics" to be found within their pages. Here is a sampling of their recommendations:[5]

Revenge strategies should be so fast and clean that the victim doesn't even notice until he walks out of his office and wonders whose blood is seeping all over the carpet.

But let's say you really hate someone, and you have a . . . reason to take her out. If you're going to do it, do it well. Be relentless. Embarrass her repeatedly. . . . One of the best places to do this is in meetings.

You can make someone crazy by doing something as apparently insignificant as taking a day to return a phone call. Or, in mid conversation, stop looking into [someone's] eyes and focus your vision elsewhere. Within seconds he'll be thinking, "Why isn't he looking at me? What did I do?"

No wonder we find such a proliferation of political workplaces! What all these books defend is the position that "it's just the way it is, so get used to it." But that is simply not correct. These authors only describe political environments. It's also erroneous to espouse "but that's just how people are." To the contrary, that's just how people behave in a political organization. *The End of Office Politics as Usual* rejects the notion that a political work environment is inevitable. Its goal is to reform office politics and remake the entire organization into a single, high-functioning team.

What You'll Find in This Book

What made W. Edwards Deming a household name (at least if your house is located on the campus of a leading business school) was the revolution in quality management that he spearheaded. He turned the business world upside down with one revolutionary concept: It's the system, not the man.

Until Deming began to focus on quality, most companies blamed any problem in the company on a person. If defects were high, you needed to fix the blame on an individual. Then you told him or her to correct it, using threats if need be. This approach sounds simple enough, but a lot of people were getting blamed for things they couldn't control and wound up spending more time covering up problems than correcting them.

Then Deming came along. He insisted most quality problems are systemic. He directed companies to fix the *system* that produced the errors, not the people. He was right.

We're going to take the same approach here. We want to fix the system that gives rise to office politics and the enemy within, not the individual players. We'll see that people act in their own best interests (no surprise there), and the rules of the game dictate how those interests are best served. It's a simple message: Change the rules, not the people.

To solve any problem, including office politics, you need first to understand its causes. As the old adage goes, A problem once defined is half solved. *The End of Office Politics as Usual* will isolate the workplace environments that tend to breed office politics. It will then define the new workplace rules, policies, and procedures to mitigate office politics and to renew the vital sense of trust and focus to make a company successful.

If any of this work sounds abstract, I assure you it's anything but. Most books that aim to transform the workplace spend most of their time espousing "values and norms" but fail to address the actual policies and procedures, such as planning and performance appraisals, that govern the workings of an organization. That isn't the case here.

The End of Office Politics as Usual provides a framework to understand your organization's political machinations and the impact they have on you personally as well as on the overall success of the enterprise. Beyond that, this book supplies a prescription for a new management system that will significantly reform office politics in your organization and refocus it on the success of the enterprise and everyone in it. That's the essence of a team-based approach.

Actual experience beats abstract theory every time. In the following pages you'll discover what we learned by observing our clients' profound experiences, by listening to people just like you in twenty-four focus groups held around the country, and by conducting an intensive two-year research effort with our alliance partners in industry and academia.

After the individual chapters in part 1 of this book, you will meet some interesting people. Ensuring anonymity, we spent literally hundreds of hours interviewing executives and distilling their personal encounters with the enemy within.

While nearly everyone had experience with office politics and the enemy within, some confided that they themselves had been the perpetrators. We found these stories the most fascinating, because they enabled us to examine the motivation and perspective of political behavior and the institutional dynamics that permit or even encourage it. These enlightening and unsettling vignettes illuminate the dynamics of a political work environment.

The second half of the book describes exactly how to rewrite the rules of the workplace. We'll examine the core systems and processes that govern any enterprise—such as goal setting, performance reviews, and resource allocation—and modify them to refocus the organization on performance. Rather than treating symptoms, our approach calls for altering an organization's basic components to encourage cooperation over masterminding, community over fiefdoms, and achieving results over positioning failure.

So prepare yourself for a journey into the heart of the enemy within. You'll discover what has really been holding you and your company back all this time.

Notes

1   Rob Lebow and William L. Simon, *Lasting Change: The Shared Values That Make a Company Great* (New York: Van Nostrand Reinhold, 1997).

2 Lawrence Serven, *A Survey on Corporate Initiatives* (Stamford, Connecticut: The Buttonwood Group, 1999), 3.

3 Barbara Bailey Reinhold, *Toxic Work: How to Overcome Stress, Overload, and Burnout & Revitalize Your Career* (New York: Dutton Books 1996), 2.

4 Lawrence Serven, *Value Planning: The New Approach to Building Value Every Day* (New York: John Wiley & Sons, 1998).

5 Ronna Lichtenberg, *Work Would Be Great if It Weren't for the People* (New York: Hyperion Press, 1998).

Karen's Story

CASE STUDY: A woman about to go on maternity leave is concerned that her job will be eliminated.

POLITICAL RESPONSE: She undermines the credibility of the person most likely to take her position.

Karen H. was a thirty-one-year-old finance professional working for a large consumer products company in the Chicago area. Karen's job as a manager of business planning was to support a product-marketing group in understanding and forecasting their product financials. To do her job well, she needed to spend time with marketing people to understand their plans, what their expected results were, and so on.

Karen worked for her company for nearly eight years and felt comfortable and established. She didn't always enjoy her job, but on balance she found working with the marketing people to be fun and exciting. Trouble began when the company hired an outsider into a key role that threatened Karen, or so she thought.

Tom J. was brought in, so everyone was told, to coordinate the results of the marketing forecasts that the business planners developed and to take more of a total company view. At first, Karen thought nothing of this new development, because people came and went every week. But after a coworker expressed suspicion that there was more to the story than what people were being told, Karen grew nervous.

"My thinking was that the company had gotten along just fine without this position for years, so why would they need to hire someone now?" Karen explained. "Why did they need to bring in an outsider? Couldn't they find anyone capable inside the company? Was this person just being hired into some type of holding-pattern job until he could be moved into the job that he was really hired for—my job?"

Karen felt justified in her concerns. After all, management did not communicate much about Tom or the job he was to fill, and in the absence of any real information, the grapevine worked overtime. Moreover, Karen was scheduled to go on maternity leave about three months after Tom was hired, and the company's human resources policy guar-

Karen's Story (continued)

anteed only that the company would hold a comparable job for her return. Karen wondered whether Tom was hired to replace her during her absence.

"There was just too much mystery and confusion about this new hire," Karen told us. "I had to do something to protect my position. After all, I'm not rich, and I couldn't afford to lose my job."

Karen decided to act. Although she didn't have a set plan, she knew what she needed to do. She needed to undermine any confidence that people might have had in Tom.

As she told the story, "I knew it wouldn't be that hard given the fact that he was new, and people tend to be suspicious of 'the new guy' anyway. In any case, the financial reporting and processes at the company are bizarre and almost impossible to figure out without experienced help, which I could withhold without him even knowing it. If this all sounds very methodical and planned out, it really wasn't. I just had a good sense of what it would take to undermine confidence in somebody, and I figured that situations would come up sooner or later. All I had to do was take advantage of them when they did."

Karen's first opportunity came sooner than she had anticipated—Tom's first day, in fact. Karen and a group of her colleagues were eating lunch together, and somebody brought up having seen "the new guy" and looked around the table for a reaction. Nobody wanted to be the first one to pass judgment on Tom since that judgment might run counter to what the rest of the group thought.

"I just wrinkled my nose, and that was enough to get 'em thinking," Karen said.

Karen had been with the company longer than most of her peers, was known as a "roll your sleeves up" manager, and had a reputation for being tough. She was respected—and feared by some—for all of these reasons. People thought twice before disputing her, especially when it came to her judgment of a coworker. Just by wrinkling her nose, nothing more, Karen signaled the group that the new guy had not impressed her. It didn't matter what the circumstances were, or if someone else would have reached the same conclusion if he had witnessed whatever she had. Karen had passed judgment, and nothing would be gained by opposing her.

"Then someone laughed and said, 'Well, looks like they picked another winner, huh?' That was exactly what I was looking for," Karen explained. "I shrugged my shoulders and changed the subject. The point had been made, no use belaboring it. I didn't want to leave anyone with the impression that I was somehow 'out to get' the new guy. That would work against me."

What Karen was doing was planting the seed of a negative reputation. "I figured out a long time ago that once a person gets a reputation people will see whatever that person does in that light, and then it becomes reinforcing." She continued, "Like, if a person developed a reputation for being a braggart, for example, people would take his mentioning that he bought a new car as bragging, reinforcing the perception. Someone who developed the general reputation for being, sarcastically speaking, 'a real winner,' eventually can do nothing right. This was what I was aiming for with Tom."

As a new employee, Tom made efforts to talk with people and try to get to know them, even staying late at the office to catch up on the work he was not able to get to during the day. "So I would say something like, 'It's nice that some people around here don't have enough to do that they can sit around socializing all day,'" Karen confessed. "Since most people left the office before Tom, nobody knew that he worked late; all they saw [was] his socializing." Unwittingly, Tom reinforced the reputation Karen had nurtured for him.

Given the Byzantine nature of the company's financial systems, Tom needed education and assistance in understanding them. Karen made herself unavailable for such assistance, and given the well-placed seeds of doubt she had planted, nobody else volunteered to help Tom, either. "I knew what he didn't know, where he was vulnerable," Karen said. "I wouldn't do it a lot, not enough to make it really noticeable, but when the right people were in the room, I'd ask Tom a question he couldn't answer. Sometimes I would jump back in and make like I was trying to find an answer for his sake. He'd look pathetic."

Karen knew enough to ease off when she heard other people make the same negative comments about Tom that she had been making.

Karen's Story (continued)

Once the momentum began to build, she stepped out of the way to watch what would happen.

Karen saw an opportunity to "put the stake in his heart" when Tom had to explain to all the managers a series of budget cuts that had been directed by senior management. She said, "Most people here don't know any better, so I made it seem that Tom had actually been the one to cut the budgets. Since he wasn't liked to begin with, that wasn't too difficult to do. After that nobody would talk to him."

Lacking any support from his colleagues and facing hostility from other managers in the company, Tom decided that he was no longer effective in his job. He left the company before he hit his two-year anniversary.

Karen, however, enhanced her reputation as "someone not to be messed with." She felt more comfortable about her position after Tom left, because the perceived threat to her job was gone. She also realized that she held sway over people's careers, that she could do it all again if necessary, and that everyone knew it.

Let's examine Karen's motivation for her political behavior and the cause behind it.

TYPE OF POLITICAL BEHAVIOR: Undermining another person's credibility.

IMPAIRMENT TO THE COMPANY: The training and development of a new executive as well as his ability to form and maintain effective working relationships.

PERSONAL MOTIVATION: Fear and uncertainty.

CONTRIBUTING WEAK INSTITUTIONAL DYNAMICS: Closed communication, lack of clear direction, and performance judged by other than goal achievement.

EFFECT ON THE COMPANY'S PROFITS: Additional recruiting and training expenses, loss of productivity, brain drain.

DEBRIEFING

Karen felt threatened by a new employee. She feared that she might lose her job, and she did what she thought was necessary to protect it, even to the point of causing another person to quit.

But let's dig a little deeper. Why did Karen feel threatened?

Karen didn't feel safe in her job even before Tom arrived; in fact she felt that her job could be taken away in a moment's notice. The rules in her company were unclear about how to advance or how to keep a job. In that case, anything could happen. Her boss and others made the rules even murkier by not speaking candidly. In this environment, then, workers only look out for their own self-interests.

For Karen or anyone else to have confidence while performing a job—a true a sense of control, worth, and contribution—that person needs to understand three elements about his or her company: the goals of the organization, or what it truly needs to achieve; the role he or she plays and the importance of that individual contribution; and the consequences for meeting or not meeting specific goals. The company's end result is a management system that can reward people based on merit.

Karen's company did not make any of these elements clear. She didn't know her company's goals (if, in fact, there were any), and she didn't know how she personally contributed to meeting those goals. Furthermore, without an objective performance evaluation process, Karen could never be certain where she stood. If her boss simply wanted her out, Karen didn't have an unequivocal performance record with which she could challenge him. This environment produces widespread, if not openly acknowledged, anxiety and self-protective behavior (which tends to feed on itself).

As a result, Karen focused not on achievements but on protecting her job. Instead of directing her energies toward accomplishing important goals for herself and her company, she undermined a colleague. She saw this action as being in her own best interests, and given the institutional dynamics of her company, nothing directed her to do otherwise.

The same environment that made Karen feel threatened was also the root of Tom's undoing. Tom had no objective way to measure his

[handwritten margin notes: "watch for in inter-view", "int"]

Karen's Story (continued)

performance. He had neither any specific and measurable goals that fed into larger company goals nor an unambiguous understanding of his role as it related to the larger organization. His job became something of a personality contest, which he lost when the managers became enraged that he had "just decided" to cut their budgets.

In short, the company's institutional dynamics that govern individual self-interest—the "manual" that lets people know what the likely consequences of their actions will be—gave rise to both Karen's behavior and its consequences for Tom. Can you think of a situation in which someone's reputation was intentionally undermined in your company?

PART I

Understanding Office Politics

CHAPTER 1

The Personal Cost of Office Politics

The Link Between Workplace Stress and Health

It's about a search . . . for daily meaning as well as daily bread, for recognition as well as cash, for astonishment rather than torpor; in short, for a life rather than a Monday through Friday sort of dying. —STUDS TERKEL

What's the personal cost to you of working in a political workplace? Any cost to your organization as a whole—be it measured in dollars, productivity, or lost opportunities—is an abstraction. You'll find that your cost, however, is not abstract at all. It's as real as migraines, lowered immune systems, and early heart attacks. It's as real as life itself—in this case, *your* life.

Black Monday Syndrome

Statistically speaking, did you know that more people have heart attacks and strokes on Mondays, between eight and nine o'clock in the morning, than at any other time during the week? To describe this relationship between cardiovascular emergencies and workplace stress, doctors have coined the term *Black Monday Syndrome.*[1]

Bertil Gardell, a leading researcher who has studied workplace stress extensively, is blunt: "An important conclusion that can be drawn from [all] these studies is that job-related stress can cause morbidity and premature death."[2] Premature death?

Harold Bloomfield agrees, saying,

Mortality rises sharply among people with prolonged stress. If you experience distress only occasionally, it will do little damage. But if you experience excessive long-term stress on a daily basis, it will profoundly disturb your health. Chronic stress can contribute to serious illness, such as heart disease or cancer.[3]

While death is surely the ultimate price to pay for workplace stress, less debilitating physical problems are much more common. They're so prevalent, in fact, that according to the American Academy of Family Physicians, two-thirds of all office visits are prompted by stress-related symptoms.

Some people believe that if they eat well and exercise they don't have to worry about stress affecting their health. Others mistakenly believe that if they are mentally tough, they can simply "gut it out."

I wish managing stress was just a matter of somehow dealing with it through the day and maybe blowing off steam at night. If only it were that simple! But our bodies react in ways that we cannot always control, especially when under stress.

Here's what happens inside your body when you experience any kind of stress, be it workplace related or otherwise. First, a section of your brain called the amygdala (you can think of it as an alarm center) signals the pituitary gland, which sends hormonal messages to the adrenal glands. At the moment they sense those hormones, the adrenals secrete adrenaline. You're thinking, *Hey, adrenaline, that's the stuff that can make a ninety-eight-pound woman lift a car off of her child, right? That stuff doesn't sound so bad.* The problem is that excess adrenaline can tear your arteries' walls, leaving places for blood fats to collect.

Next, if the stress is prolonged, your body enters what's called the resistance stage, and the pituitary gland secretes more hormones. One of these hormones, vasopressin, constricts your arteries, raising your blood pressure. (This reaction permits more blood to go to the muscles and brain and reduces the risk of severe blood loss. Your body thinks it's fight-or-flight time). Another hormone, adrenocorticotropin, or more commonly ACTH, further activates your adrenal glands to produce cortisol, which raises your blood sugar level and alters your immune system. It also increases blood-clotting elements, which adhere to your artery walls and narrow them.

The third and final stage of the stress response is physical exhaustion. It's the primary complaint heard in doctor's offices. (You probably could have guessed that.) Signs of chronic fatigue include a lowered attention span, a decreased sex drive, insomnia and waking up tired, irritability and temper outbursts, a pasty and pale complexion, and impaired short-term memory. Chronic stress can lead to increased cholesterol levels; excess secretion of stomach acid, which can lead to peptic ulcers; greater plaque formation in the arteries; and increased heart rate and electrical conduction problems, which can cause cardiac arrhythmia.[4] As Bloomfield told us, mortality does rise sharply among people with prolonged stress.

A Personal Story

One of the women interviewed for this book, Pam W., recounted her years with the enemy within and the impact they had on her health. Here, in her own words, is her story.

"In retrospect a lot about where I used to work seems so clear to me, but at the time nothing was. We were in a dysfunctional situation; everything was based on politics—who owed who and who was out to get who. It was much more important *who* you were than what you thought or did. From my perspective, the whole point seemed to be just to stay out of trouble, to avoid being blamed.

"The real upshot working there was that you needed to pay more attention to what other people thought and less attention to what you thought. You needed to be guarded about what you said and did just to stay in good graces with the company and the people in it.

"It was out of control, but I thought I wasn't touched just because I wasn't on anybody's shit list and I didn't have one of my own. But I'd wake up feeling tired. I was jumpy even at home and really irritable with my kids. They just couldn't seem to do anything right in my mind. The weird thing was that my eyesight began to deteriorate. I never had a problem before—I played field hockey in college—but within a year I was nearsighted and needed glasses. The worst thing, though, was I just couldn't seem to concentrate when I needed to, and everything took me twice as long as it should have.

"Yet even with all that going on I still didn't pay much attention to my health. It wasn't until I discovered I had an ulcer at age forty-one that I knew I was in big trouble. My dad and his friends had ulcers. That was never supposed to happen to us! That's when I woke up and realized that my life at work could take away my real life, and how could that ever be worth it? Right? So I left and went back to my old company, even though it meant a cut in pay. I can't even begin to describe how much better I feel today, and I still can't believe I gave up five years of my life to that craziness."

Although Pam's story is unique, her reaction to a stressful workplace is common. Others, too, have suffered physically from the effects of workplace stress, but where does this stress come from? Could it come from the job itself, or does it come from other factors? What role does office politics play?

The Workplace Stress of Air Traffic Controllers

If anyone suffers from workplace stress, it has to be air traffic controllers. They're personally responsible for literally hundreds of human lives during every shift. One small mistake could mean the loss of someone's spouse or child. Of course, they all experience workplace stress. It's endemic in their job, right? Wrong.

In 1978 researcher Dr. MacBride studied air traffic controllers (ATCs) with the goal of mitigating workplace stress.[5] What MacBride found surprised her. Only 10 percent of the ATCs she studied displayed chronic stress symptoms. She analyzed this group's demographic and personality characteristics and found nothing that distinguished them from their colleagues. Nor did she find anything unique about their job activities or how they performed their jobs.

Okay, they did the same work, had the same background, and shared personality traits, but what made these ATCs different? Why was one group of ATCs experiencing chronic stress and not the other 90 percent?

MacBride discovered that the people who experienced chronic stress had been managed differently. They had frequently complained about organizational structure and management practices that interfered with their career advancement, with their participation in decision making, and with their communications with management. More extensive investigations proved that most of the ATCs' complaints were, in fact, well grounded.

In most situations, workplace stress isn't caused by something inherently stressful about the work itself, but rather the environment in which the work is performed. A political work environment is a breeding ground for stress. We'll take a look at why that's the case here.

Not Knowing Is What Will Kill You

Moviemakers have known for decades the secret to scaring the daylights out of their audiences. It involves the psychology of fear. If we are aware of a threat, such as a grizzly bear, and we can see it, then we can act appropriately to survive. We can watch exactly where the bear roams so we don't get any closer to it, we can determine how large a threat it actually is, and finally we can decide the best course of action for survival. Without actually seeing the threat, however, we would not be able to make any determination that would improve our chances of survival.

In the psychology of fear, it is the unidentified threat that induces the most fear and stress. Moviemakers have used this knowledge successfully for decades. It's the reason why we didn't actually see the shark in the entire first half of the classic movie *Jaws*, and even after that we only caught mere glimpses of the beast.

Jim Schadt is an industry leader and seasoned executive who knows something about anxiety and challenges. Among other accomplishments, as chief executive officer (CEO) of *Reader's Digest*, he helped steer the company from a closely held business to a publicly traded company on the New York Stock Exchange. Yet Schadt admits he also had his share of losses and personal defeats. Like all effective leaders, he culls the important lessons he learned from all of his experiences, both the good and bad. Jim often counsels people that through the ups and downs he's concluded that "the hardest thing is not knowing where you stand."

Schadt is not alone in his thinking. Workplace studies show that next to out-and-out abrasive behavior, ambiguity creates the most tension. When people are unsure of the rules, they become confused, setting off a cycle of ongoing mistrust.[6]

Per Schadt's point, if you want to know where you stand in the workplace, you have to know three things: (1) What needs to be accomplished? (2) What is your role in achieving that goal? (3) What is in it for you?

Knowing these three answers enables you first to anticipate whether you're likely to succeed and to prepare yourself as best you can. Then once you've begun to work towards your goal, you can determine whether you're making progress and whether you're actually succeeding. Finally, when you've accomplished your goals, you'll feel as if you've contributed to something larger than yourself. However, not knowing the answers to *all three* questions leaves you in the anxious position of wondering where you stand.

Can you answer all three questions about your job today?

When people don't know where they stand in a political organization, they become confused and anxious, and they quickly engage in a whole host of self-protective behaviors. When people become fearful, they join in the political fray.

The Fear Factor

Harold Geneen is a revered name in management circles. During his tenure as CEO of ITT (1959–1977), he engineered one of the most successful business stories in history. Known as a tough, no-nonsense manager, Geneen had little tolerance for excuses. Yet he nonetheless recognized the importance of keeping fear out of the workplace:

> *To the degree that business commanders strike fear in the hearts of their management team, they have turned the American busi-*

ness world into a jungle in which scared people compete within a company for their own personal survival. In the long run I am certain this is counterproductive. First of all, frightened people play office politics; *they won't come forward and admit there's a problem early enough to be solved.*[7] *(Emphasis added.)*

MM
-ED

In a politically dominated workplace, people frankly have many reasons to be afraid. Without clear rules, they fear:

- Being labeled as boat rockers or as not team players

- Not fitting in with the organization

- Losing their self-esteem, including being humiliated in front of others

- Missing advancement opportunities

- Losing their jobs

- Forfeiting their credibility and reputations

This last fear—losing one's credibility—is perhaps the most prevalent in a political environment, given that undermining a colleague's credibility is a common tactic for maintaining one's position. This machination proves so effective because it is usually done in secret and the unwitting target cannot defend herself. Thus, the loss of her credibility is usually permanent.

MM

"I've seen this happen so many times," one participant told us, "and sometimes it's triggered just because someone spoke up and said what they thought was right. Behind the scenes they take that person apart. I know, I've been in those meetings. People learn that these subtle repercussions can really hurt you, and they should watch out for it. It becomes kind of a background stress that's always there, and people have their guard up. They know that if you say something you shouldn't it will come back to haunt you, unpredictably, sometimes unrecognizably to all but a few who really know."

This admission illustrates the double bind created for workers who want to do the right thing and contribute their best, for those who might recognize the truth and want to address it but need to avoid offending the wrong people. They might be reluctant to speak up for a rational reason: The work environment might not be safe for telling the truth. This fear of subtle and indirect repercussions is a form of covert bullying to keep people in line.

Yet the bullies aren't the only ones who keep the political machine going. Even the victims contribute to the status quo when they avoid confronting those political behaviors that hamper trust, mutual respect, and team building. Driven by fear, their passive acceptance of these circumstances allows the political workplace to perpetuate.

Political workplaces tend to breed fear. That fact, and all its repercussions, is a major source of work stress. Yet it is only one way that a political environment can induce stress.

Loss of Control

At the landmark conference "Work Stress and the Role of Health Care Delivery Systems," researchers looked at such work setting considerations as autonomy, institutional goals, leadership, and social isolation. They discovered that people who felt isolated, devoid of leadership, and disconnected from or unaware of institutional goals experienced markedly more stress on the job. These conditions are all recognizable hallmarks of a political work environment.

Autonomy, the first consideration in the researchers' list, turns out to be the most pivotal requirement for workplace satisfaction. According to Robert Karasek, a leading researcher in this field, a worker's worst scenario is when he faces *high demands* (which most of us do) coupled with *low control* over how he meets those demands. When people have little opportunity to use their own judgment in fulfilling their work requirements or in varying the pace of their activities, they face greater risks of physical affliction.[8] That's the identical conclusion reached in the famous Framingham Heart Study. Doctors found that the people most likely to have heart disease had jobs that carried high demands but offered little autonomy.[9]

What exactly, though, is the connection between a lack of autonomy and workplace stress? Working conditions that seriously constrain workers' self-determination and opportunities for using their creativity conflict with fundamental human needs relating to their self-esteem and their need to control their environment. Self-doubt, frustration, and anger follow. In the absence of self-directedness, people feel hemmed in and pierced by a lack of fulfillment. If they can't influence and shape their own workday, they lose confidence in themselves, and eventually they lose interest in work altogether—apart from their paychecks.

How does a political workplace contribute to this lack of autonomy? Remember that autonomy means *the goals or outcomes of a person's work are clearly defined, and the means to achieve them rest with the worker.* She can manage her own assignments and feel a certain freedom of movement to accomplish her goals.

In a political work environment, management never clearly defines its goals and forever changes them. Workers have no opportunity to "go for it," because the "it" is rarely defined. Instead, workers must respond to their superiors' shifting needs and desires. Some participants in our study referred to this situation as being "in constant fire-fighting mode."

Even when goals *are* defined in a political organization, workers rarely experience free rein to meet them. As previously illustrated, people working in a political environment spend much of their time looking over their shoulders, and ensuring that their backsides are covered and that they haven't offended anybody important. Whatever solution they propose to meet their goals needs to be politically correct, which can feel even more restrictive than an autocratic supervisor's tight grip.

Stress Buffers in Political Organizations

The *work stress* conference concluded that the quality of workers' interpersonal relationships, whether with superiors or colleagues, is a strong determinant of workplace stress. If their relationships are supportive and based on a foundation of trust, they can be a major stress buffer. People who enjoy strong support from work mates can cope with changes and difficulties in their jobs. If work relationships are adversarial and devoid of trust, however, then they actually become another source of stress.[10]

In a political organization, are interpersonal relationships a source of stress or a stress buffer? In our research, we learned that interpersonal relationships are strained in political organizations and serve as a primary contributor to workers' stress. Even the small handful of people who consider themselves "winners" in the political fray never allow themselves to get close enough to their colleagues to form supportive relationships.

Tying It Together: The Impact on Work Life

Employees working in a growth-oriented, successful, and well-managed organization expend much less effort in coping with stress than those in a political work environment. Our research, which is consistent with other major studies, in fact, shows that people in well-managed organizations experience completely different feelings than people in political workplaces (see figure 1-1).

The impact office politics has on work life can be debilitating. Given the conditions described throughout this chapter, people working in these environments experience coercion, monotony, mental strain, and social isolation. They often feel powerless, regard their job as meaningless, and see no value in their work other than the money they earn.[11]

W. Edwards Deming, the father of the Total Quality Movement, put it this way: "A man dare not take a risk. He must guard his own security; it is safer to stay in line."[12]

This type of passivity, which can be a matter of survival in a political

FIGURE 1-1
The Differences Between How People Feel in Well-Managed and Politically Dominant Organizations

HOW PEOPLE IN WELL-MANAGED ORGANIZATIONS FEEL	HOW PEOPLE IN POLITICALLY DOMINANT ORGANIZATIONS FEEL
Competent	Anxious
Interested	Controlled
Clear	Confused
Comfortable	Angry
Fulfilled	Invisible
Excited	Empty
Trusting	Manipulated
Strong	Fearful
Happy	Used

organization, drains people of their natural creativity and enthusiasm. They become less inclined to get involved in the process of making changes, even ones that might improve their own working conditions.

Yet even when people "check out" in a political organization, they usually don't give up completely. Even while experiencing alienation, spirit-cracking boredom, and work that mocks their human capacity, internally they know they are capable of so much more. This conflict between human potential and the stifling grip of a politically dominated work environment is what destroys motivation and an organization's ability to succeed.

Building on this understanding, in chapter 2 we will closely examine the many negative effects of office politics on the organization as a whole. We will especially focus on office politics as they relate to a company's ability to perform in an increasingly competitive landscape.

Notes

1 Health, Education, and Welfare Department, *Work in America: Report of a Special Task Force to the U.S. Department of Health, Education, and Welfare* (Cambridge, Mass.: MIT Press, 1973).

2 Bertil Gardell, "Efficiency and Health Hazards in Mechanized Work," in *Work Stress: Health Care Systems in the Workplace,* eds. James Quick, Rabi Bhagat, James Dalton, and Jonathan Quick (New York: Praeger Publishers, 1987).

3 Harold Bloomfield, M.D., *Healing Anxiety With Herbs* (New York: HarperCollins, 1998), 53.

4 Ibid., 52.

5 James C. Quick et al., eds., *Work Stress: Health Care Systems in the Workplace* (New York: Praeger Publishers, 1987), 41.

6 Kathleen D. Ryan, *Driving Fear out of the Workplace* (San Francisco: Jossey-Bass, 1998), 66.

7 Harold Geneen and Alvin Moscow, *Managing* (Garden City, N.Y.: Doubleday 1984), 145.

8 Barbara Bailey Reinhold, *Toxic Work: How to Overcome Stress, Overload, and Burnout and Revitalize Your Career* (New York: Dutton Books, 1996), 22.

9 S. G. Haynes, "Type A Behavior, Employment Status, and Coronary Heart Disease in Women," *Behavioral Medicine Update* 6 (4): 11–15 (1987).

10 James Quick, Rabi Bhagat, James Dalton, and Jonathan Quick, eds., *Work Stress: Health Care Systems in the Workplace* (New York: Praeger, 1987), 64.

11 Ibid., 52.

12 W. Edwards Deming, *Out of the Crisis* (Cambridge, Mass.: MIT Center for Advanced Engineering Study, 1982).

Steve's Story

CASE STUDY: An aggressive marketing manager wants to improve his odds of being promoted.

POLITICAL RESPONSE: He reduces the number of perceived competitors for promotion.

This story is one of the more disturbing ones in this book, for reasons that will soon be obvious. While it describes an extreme case of what can only be described as dysfunctional behavior, it illustrates what can go wrong when a company focuses more on personalities than results.

Meet Steve S., a young and aggressive marketing manager for a large consumer electronics company. Out of business school for just four years, he has already been promoted twice, along with about a third of the product managers that started at the same time he did.

He has learned that in his company being promoted is more a game of elimination than of selection. Here's how he explained it.

"Every year the executive management of the division meets to decide what product managers should make it to the next level," Steve began. "Every once in a while one of the senior executives will feel very good about a candidate and really push for his or her promotion. But that doesn't happen very often. It sounds a little strange, but the real question isn't so much, Why should we promote this guy? but rather, Why shouldn't we promote him? More often than not people speak up only when they feel someone shouldn't get promoted. Then unless someone sticks his neck out to defend the guy—again, unlikely—he's just passed over.

"It's pretty simple really. If you're a senior executive there's a risk of strongly backing some guy up only to have another senior executive shoot him down. Yet there's almost no risk to saying that you don't like someone. Of course, nobody comes right out and says, 'I just don't like this guy, he rubs me the wrong way.' They say things like, 'Bob isn't a team player,' or, 'Sally doesn't inspire confidence.' The trick, if you're a product manager looking for the next promotion, is to avoid giving someone a reason not to like you. It's so simple that most people just don't get it."

Steve's Story (continued)

Normally people take much longer than Steve did to figure out this kind of promotion process, but he drew from another experience. "I know this might sound funny, but it's not all that different from the days in my fraternity," he informed us. "I mean, back then, during rush, if someone didn't like you, then there's no way you'd get in. Not that anyone was looking for a reason not to like someone, but if you wound up rubbing someone the wrong way, forget it. So I'd tell the guys I really liked not to worry so much about impressing anyone; that's normally where you get into trouble. Instead, just hang back, don't get too flashy, and you'd slide right in."

For all the outward signs of professionalism in Steve's company (they still hadn't gone to casual dress even as this book went to press), the dynamics were pretty much the same as in his fraternity. "One of the guys in our IT [information technology] department is from Australia, and he calls it 'the tall poppy syndrome,'" Steve said. "I guess the tall poppies are the first ones to get cut."

Steve's clear advantage was that he understood this dynamic far better than any of his peers. He observed that many of his peers overreached, or simply tried too hard to impress the higher-ups, and in doing so often wound up offending somebody in some way. Steve, however, observed that doing a "good" job without rubbing anyone the wrong way was much more effective than ever trying to do a "great" job. Many of his peers didn't understand this strategy and were too eager to hit the ball out of the park. Steve enjoyed watching them go to bat.

But even at this early stage in his career, Steve could see the promotion pyramid getting narrower. In the beginning, it was enough to let people shoot themselves in the foot and be passed over for promotion. But as he scaled the pyramid, he perceived that his competition grew more serious. He felt that he needed to become more active in helping people eliminate themselves from contention. So Steve looked for situations in which he could "encourage" one of his peers to say or do the wrong thing.

As with Karen in the previous story, Steve knew the power of asking somebody in a large meeting about something that he or she couldn't answer. He called this maneuver a "Scud" (a reference to the missile of choice used by the Iraqi army). Steve revealed, "The trick is never to overplay your hand, never let people know that you had every intent of embarrassing someone. You've got to choose your situations very carefully, otherwise everyone will be on to you and you won't ever be able to do it again without it backfiring."

Steve developed numerous tactics to undermine his colleagues, but he realized that he would have to "take it to the next level" to eliminate some of the stiffer competition in the next promotion cycle. What he chose to do was quite simple and effective. All he needed one late night was to repress his conscience.

Steve targeted Mike L. for his efforts, because he appeared most likely to get promoted and was pretty trusting. Steve also considered that by taking out the leading candidate early, he'd face less competition for promotion overall.

Steve explained, "Look, I'm not proud of what happened, but this type of thing goes on all the time in every company, I'm sure. You can't be naïve about it.

"Here's what happened. Mike had been preparing for an important meeting with the new company president for weeks. The meeting was set to cover Mike's product line and bring the new president up to speed on the history of the product, market and industry trends, the standard stuff. It was pretty well understood that the new company president was very detailed oriented and liked to talk about price points in all 120 markets and the intricacies of trade discount models. Sounded a little anal, if you ask me, but the trick to winning him over was to bring a lot of this detailed backup and be prepared to discuss it all."

Steve knew that Mike would be lost without his reports. "So the night before the big meeting," Steve continued, "I stayed late to work on a special project—at least that's what I told everyone. When everyone else had gone home, and the cleaning people had come and gone, I went over to Mike's computer and formatted his hard drive."

Formatting the hard drive erased all of Mike's files that he had

Steve's Story (continued)

stored there, including the ones he needed for his meeting with the president.

"You should have seen his face the next morning when he realized his files were gone," Steve said. "I mean I know I shouldn't laugh about this stuff, but if you had seen it, you'd know just what I'm talking about. He came over to my cube and told me his computer had crashed and was like, 'What am I gonna do, what am I gonna do!' "

Understandably, Mike was thrown off balance when he discovered that all of his data had vanished overnight, but apparently he did his best to maintain his composure when he actually met with the new president. According to Steve, "Mike told me later that he thought that he had almost managed to escape without any grilling, but he wasn't that lucky." Steve elaborated, "Apparently the company president asked about the difference in net trade discounted pricing in southern Idaho, one of the strongest regions for Mike's product. When Mike admitted that he didn't know offhand, the president asked if Mike had brought any backup material. Mike told him that he hadn't, because his computer had crashed. He said it came out sounding like, 'My dog ate my homework.' I'm sure the meeting went downhill from there."

Steve told us that later that afternoon the other product managers all talked about what bad luck Mike had had, having his computer crash the night before an important meeting. Steve joined in sympathetically, but he thought his colleagues were being hypocritical.

"I mean, deep down they were just as happy I was," Steve said. "They were celebrating his loss, believe me. At least I can be honest with myself. Survival of the fittest—let's be honest."

Let's take a closer look at Steve's motivation.

TYPE OF POLITICAL BEHAVIOR: Coworker sabotage.

IMPAIRMENT TO THE COMPANY: An executive's ability to brief properly and thoroughly the company's president.

PERSONAL MOTIVATION: Envy, blind ambition.

CONTRIBUTING WEAK INSTITUTIONAL DYNAMICS: Performance not judged by goal achievement or individual merit, but rather by comparison to others.

EFFECT ON THE COMPANY'S PROFITS: Brain drain, suboptimal decision making in regard to personnel evaluations.

DEBRIEFING

Steve's basic desire to get ahead was not unusual, but certainly his actions were highly dysfunctional and detrimental to the organization. That's an important distinction to draw, because the desire to get ahead can be motivational in the right environment.

Steve was a keen observer of how people advanced in his company. He concluded, accurately I might add, that the promotion process was based on elimination instead of selection. Steve accepted the system for what it was and worked it to his advantage.

Without going into a full case study here, Steve's company operated without any guiding force or strategy. Management did not have a system to establish goals, to offer incentives tied to meeting those goals, or to assess individual performance. As a result, its employees lacked any meaningful sense of direction or accountability for achieving results. Instead, they had to navigate a political maze, and Steve was becoming a master at it.

While Steve is a bright person, his talents are being directed toward unproductive and dysfunctional behavior. We can't help but wonder how much value Steve could generate if someone gave him the proper motivation and direction.

Have you ever suspected that somebody's work might have been undermined in your company?

CHAPTER 2

The Organizational Cost of Office Politics

The Link Between People, Decisions, and Performance

No one can put in his best performance unless he feels secure.
—W. EDWARDS DEMING

I n chapter 1, we reviewed the high *personal* costs of office politics. While it might prompt you to take action, your organization will most likely remain unmoved by the personal toll that dealing with the enemy within takes on you. Like it or not, unless you are a key employee, management probably considers you expendable.

To motivate your company to fight the enemy within, then, management must see the cost to the organization as a whole. The question you must address is simple: If we as an organization ignore office politics in our workplace, so what? Answer the question thoughtfully if you want to get management's attention and even begin to reform office politics where you work.

In this chapter, we'll address that question. We'll also provide a business case for making the necessary changes to reform office politics where you work.

The estimated productivity loss because of stress-related factors is more than $100 billion in the United States alone.[1] While that statistic alone is alarming, most companies will not be moved until they truly understand the connection between politics and performance, which we will establish in this chapter.

Just How High Can the Cost Be?
The Space Shuttle *Challenger*

After the 1986 *Challenger* explosion, NASA launched an investigation to determine its cause. The resulting testimony of the scientists and engineers who worked on the space shuttle is, in a word, chilling.

The investigators first focused on the *Challenger*'s technical dimensions and engineering specifications, what you would expect. But as they dug deeper to explain the failure of the ill-fated *Challenger,* they uncovered some all-too-human contributions that could have prevented the worst disaster in NASA's history.

The testimony showed some people who worked closely on the project had been worried about the craft's worthiness. Others just "felt" that it shouldn't be launched. The explosion of the *Challenger* space shuttle did not surprise those who worked most closely on it and had concerns.

What went wrong? Besides the technical failures, what clearly contributed to the disaster was the pressure people felt that any hold up of the shuttle's launch would be costly in many ways. They felt that the program needed to *look* successful, and a delay could ruin that image. While many people could have suggested stopping the launch, nobody wanted to face the personal ramifications for doing so. Such a call would not have been grounds for dismal, but it would have been "career limiting" nonetheless.

Do you feel the same kind of pressure to make your organization look good no matter what? For politically dominant workplaces, this kind of influence is, of course, all too familiar. Fortunately the associated costs are rarely as high as they were with the *Challenger* disaster, but these workplaces will suffer from a costly performance gap.

Living up to Potential

Every company has a gap between its *actual* performance and its *potential* performance. The level at which its workers could perform is almost always higher. Having said that, for exceptionally well-run companies, this gap is small or almost inconsequential. They've essentially closed the gap and are operating at peak performance. That ability is what makes them so admired. For the remaining 90 percent of all organizations (yours included or you wouldn't have picked up this book), this gap is significant. Working to close the performance gap, as illustrated in figure 2-1, is the only thing that will bring wealth and success to the company and its shareholders (or stakeholders for not-for-profit organizations). Now that's something any organization should care about.

As seen in figure 2-1, office politics—or the enemy within that creates a drag on organizational effectiveness—cause a portion (sometimes a large portion) of the performance gap. We'll spend the majority of this chapter explaining why and how. But suffice it to say here that office politics can undermine trust, stifle innovation, drive turnover, distort communica-

FIGURE 2-1
The Performance Gap

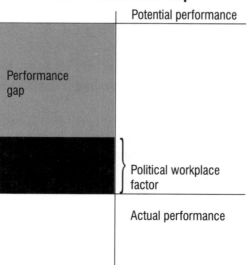

Potential performance

Performance gap

Political workplace factor

Actual performance

tions, corrode joy and pride in work, and most of all lead to bad decision making.

Carlene Ellis, Intel's vice president for organization, has wryly observed that the key to a company's success in closing the performance gap is to recognize the stupid things the company does and then find a way to stop doing them.[2] Office politics generate a whole host of wasteful behaviors, thus making them high-leverage candidates for fixing. Some friends from Deloitte Consulting put a different spin on it: "Political companies are anti-growth; they develop slow growth DNA."[3] But from whatever angle you look at it, a company's performance gap will balloon with the negative effects of office politics.

In figure 2-1 the political workplace factor explains perhaps one-third of the performance gap. In your company, it might be higher or lower, but in any case, it's most certainly the first issue that companies must address.

Decision Making in a Political Workplace

Do office politics improve the decision-making process or retard it? We believe that the enemy within is *a crippling force that inhibits an organization from being consistently profitable over time* precisely *because its office politics undermine the decision-making process.*

Every business is based on a chain of activities. Customer needs are identified, products or services are developed and delivered to meet those needs, bills are sent out and collected, and so on. Likewise, employees make dozens of business decisions in this chain every day.

In the best-managed and most successful companies that we have studied, employees' decisions are based on factual analysis and evidence (rigorously developed and lively debated) with the clear goal of maximizing shareholder wealth and the benefits to the organization as a whole. Their companies recognize that, apart from numerous disparate opinions, they need to base their decisions on facts and objective standards and debate them on the same grounds. There are specific questions that need to be answered.

Maximizing Shareholder Wealth Criteria:

Is it good for the customer?

Is it good for the organization?

Is it good for our shareholders/stakeholders?

Is it good for our employees?

While some managers might value their employees' gut feelings and intuition, these feelings still need to be supported by data and a compelling business case. In a well-run organization, facts and principles are worth more than titles and personalities. What gets people ahead here are well-reasoned, firmly grounded, and thoughtfully analyzed decisions. As a result, the right decisions are made in the best interests of the company or organization.

In a political workplace, the approach is different. Instead of maximizing wealth for the company, management promotes personal growth and prestige. People struggle to ensure the survival of their personal empires regardless of the cost to stakeholders. It boils down to answering questions like these:

Maximizing Political Capital Criteria:

Will it make powerful people look good?

Will it make powerful people look bad?

Will it make someone I don't like look good?

Will it make someone I don't like look bad?

Will it enhance my own power?

Now imagine that you're going to invest your own hard-earned money in one of two companies. Where would you want to invest it—with the company that makes its decisions based on maximizing shareholder wealth criteria or the one that makes its decisions based on maximizing political capital criteria? You should never put your money into a company that uses investments to subsidize activities, practices, and business strategies that build personal empires instead of shareholder value (unless, of course, you're looking to *lose* money).

Communications Breakdown

Knowledge is power. We've all heard that adage before, but nowhere is it more true than in a political workplace, where people build personal empires. There, no one openly shares knowledge for that would mean giving away their power. Who would be naïve enough to do that?

The high cost to an organization from restricted information flow is akin to siphoning off oxygen from the brain. It grossly impairs a company's ability to respond effectively to competitive market conditions. Yet information blocks are not the only issues that political organizations have with open communication.

To avoid conflicts that might come back to haunt them, executives in political organizations learn to abstain from straight talk in meetings. They don't say what they really mean or test other's assumptions. They follow the mistaken notion that to get along you've got to go along. The problem with this behavior is that people then never clearly resolve important issues. These defensive routines prevent people from making honest decisions; consequently, meetings end with broad smiles but without defined action.

Another communication problem found in many political organizations pertains to hiding mistakes. The enemy within is constantly searching out the weak and vulnerable, both to weed out competition and to improve one's comparative performance. They can say, "Hey, at least I didn't screw up like that other guy did." Of course, everyone is at his or her most vulnerable after making a mistake, but they are more so in a political workplace when others exploit those mistakes. Thus people learn to cover up their mistakes.

Hiding snafus takes time and other resources that could be spent more productively. Hidden problems also tend to fester and get compounded simply because they are not addressed. That's obvious. What isn't so obvious is that mistakes often provide invaluable lessons *if* people openly acknowledge and analyze them. As they say, Experience is the best teacher. But most important, openly acknowledged mistakes are rarely repeated, while hidden mistakes tend to recur with unwelcome frequency.

How People Spend Their Time

An easy way to measure the organizational cost of office politics is simply to look at how people spend their time. In the better-run companies we studied, workers spent their time solving problems, searching for opportunities, learning about their customers and their needs, and looking for ways to work smarter, faster, and better. Managers take an active role in gathering and disseminating information, developing strategies and plans, and measuring results. You'll see people acting in the organization's best interests, with which their own personal interests are purposefully aligned. Not surprising these companies so often win and reward their shareholders with an upward-trending stock price.

Look inside a political workplace, and you'll see people spending their time on something other than upholding the company's best interests. Each person on the organization chart is busy transforming his or her position into a private fiefdom, with each manager thinking only of his own piece of turf and almost nobody thinking of what's best for the company as a whole.

You'll see managers fighting off any proposed change that threatens in any way to erode their personal status, their resources, or their influence over rival executives. In this environment, you'll see subordinates coping with their bosses by "handling" them—catering to their whims and offering little debate or their own innovative ideas. They suspect that their boss's decisions are based more on personal considerations than on thoughtful analysis, and they're usually right.

In general, you'll see people acting in their own self-interests, which have almost nothing in common with the overall company's interests. It should be no surprise that these companies so often lose and disappoint their stockholders with eroding stock prices.

A Return to the Individual View

Now that we've examined the organizational impact of office politics, or the enemy within, let's briefly return to the individual worker. You can't fully understand the vicious cycle in which the workers find themselves without understanding what's happening to the individuals who work there. Here is what we have found.

The more political work becomes, the less *responsible* workers become. Instead, they grow psychologically *disconnected* from their work and learn to work just for their paycheck. They rarely put in any *extra effort* and stop taking risks and thinking creatively. Thus, they lose any *personal ownership* of their work or the results of that work.

When they feel as if they're juggling between *conflicting priorities*—those of the company, their bosses, and themselves—they approach work by just doing what they're told and hoping for a promotion. They try to stay out of the boss's way and out of trouble.[4]

When managers *lose their sense of commitment*, they begin to rationalize that they are working in a company large enough to hide and absorb numerous mistakes. They don't have to correct them. Their job simply becomes a means to something that lies outside of the company. Although the company wants people to commit, *they see little to which they can commit themselves.*

In a political environment, people learn to worry about their jobs, *not the business.* Over time, they become *numbed*, less aware, and not alert. Their problem-solving potential erodes.

In this vicious cycle, eventually people who don't feel responsible simply show up in the morning, *halfheartedly do what they're told*, and go home.

Just take any three points listed above and ask yourself, How can people in this environment make good, effective decisions? The answer is they can't on any consistent basis, and that's what brings us full circle. Ultimately, an organization is only as good as the decisions its people make. Anything, including office politics, that diminishes or obstructs their ability to make effective decisions must be remedied for a company to succeed.

Notes

1   James Quick, "Preventing Stress Intervention: A Challenging Area for Researchers," in *Work Stress: Health Care Systems in the Workplace,* James

Quick, Rabi Bhagat, James Dalton, and Jonathan Quick, eds. (New York: Praeger Publishers, 1987), 151.

2 Sally Helgesen, *The Web of Inclusion* (New York: Doubleday, 1995), 64.

3 Thomas L. Doorley and John M. Donovan, *Value-Creating Growth* (San Francisco: Jossey-Bass, 1999), 77.

4 John Case, *Open-Book Management* (New York: HarperBusiness, 1996), 51.

Frank's Story

CASE STUDY: A plant manager gets angry when a young executive from headquarters uncovers productivity problems.

POLITICAL RESPONSE: The manager works to get him fired.

Frank M. had been a plant manager for a leading soft drink beverage company for fifteen years when we met him. He had almost complete autonomy and control of his plant, aside from a couple of annual visits from the corporate chieftains. The plant was his domain, and things were done his way. Frank had the last word on everything, from the color of the paint used on the handrails around the plant, to the number of overtime hours worked on any given Saturday, to the monthly menu changes in the cafeteria. The plant is officially known as the Little Beaverton plant because of its Kentucky location, but the employees call it "Frank's World." Here's his story.

"Two years ago my company hired a consulting firm to help figure out ways to reduce turnover in the executive ranks," Frank said. "One of the recommendations they made for job enrichment was to rotate executives through a variety of functions. I guess the thinking was people needed to move around the company more, even spending time in other functional areas. So an engineer, for example, might do a stint in plant operations or even marketing. The idea was to give people a broader view of the company, do some cross training, and make a career at the cola company more interesting. The program was called START—sharing talent and resources together."

Frank had heard about this program, but he did not think it would involve his plant, at least not immediately. He was wrong. He explained, "I got a call from the director of U.S. operations, who was my boss, telling me that an engineering executive from headquarters would be spending a year or two at the Little Beaverton Plant as part of the START program. I was more than a little unhappy about the thought of having a headquarters spy at my plant.

"I told Bill that I thought this START program sounded great," Frank recounted, "but I didn't think Little Beaverton was the right

Frank's Story (continued)

plant to do it in. We only produce a couple of the brands, and all of them are still batch processed the old-fashioned way. I suggested they do this thing with the Puerto Rico plant instead, since they have the new processing technology and they do twice as many flavors as we do."

But Frank's boss made it clear that he had made up his mind. So Frank resigned himself, grudgingly, to the idea of "babysitting" a headquarters executive for awhile.

"Two weeks before the new executive was expected to arrive at the Little Beaverton plant," Frank continued, "I announced it at my weekly staff meeting. There was a lot of groaning around the table, which was just what I had expected."

Plant employees were generally suspicious of people from head-quarters, and they often referred to them as spies. The pervasive belief was that people from headquarters could offer little help and frequently just got underfoot.

"I was glad to see that they were upset about it, or I would have been a little worried otherwise," Frank admitted. "I remember telling them that we should give this guy an office in the back of the plant, away from the rest of us, let him tinker around a bit, and go back to headquarters in a year just as if he was never really here."

Everyone agreed on Frank's approach to the problem, but he had to establish one more point. "I told them one other thing, and I put it in plain English. I told them that I would tear them a new one if any of them gave this guy anything other than the time of day. The last thing we needed around there was some idiot from headquarters trying to change things. Everyone got it."

*   *   *

Tony D. had spent five years at headquarters working in the company's engineering department. He had shown real promise, as Frank later found out, and was selected to join the first group of people to partici-pate in the START program. Although he was flattered at being chosen, he apparently had some reservations about spending a year in Little Beaverton. He told Frank after he had been there awhile that he had not been that keen on leaving New York, which he loved. He knew what the opportunity could mean for his career, though, and he decided to make the best of it.

"Tony spent much of his first week just settling in, finding a place to live, learning his way around the plant," Frank recalled. "Everyone he met was polite enough, but I'm sure they all seemed to be in a hurry to go somewhere else." Frank smiled. "Only Edgar, his direct boss at the plant, spent much time with him. I'm sure that even then a lot of topics appeared to be off-limits."

Tony eventually did settle in, and he even joined a local softball league. His role at the plant was to run the capital appropriations process, formalizing requests for new equipment for headquarters' approval. He was also expected to lend his expertise to ensure the product lines ran smoothly and efficiently. That's where the trouble started.

To do a good job, Tony needed to understand how the products were manufactured, which turned out to be a challenge. "Nobody wanted to talk to him about it, or when they did they would talk in such broad, sweeping terms that they might as well have said nothing at all," Frank explained. "It was all part of the program to keep him isolated, and it was working."

Tony was tenacious, however, spending time on the factory floor and speaking with the hourly workers who operated the machinery. He learned more from them than he had speaking to the director of manufacturing. Eventually Tony discovered something that Frank had been hiding from headquarters for years.

*   *   *

"Tony went looking for problems and he found some, okay?" Frank seemed irritated recalling this part of the story. "He learned that productivity in the Little Beaverton plant was lower than in any of the other plants in the company on a comparative basis, and as a consequence, our production costs were higher. What had masked this fact was that the raw materials' costs were lower than in the other plants, so the total cost to produce our products was similar to any other plant in the system.

"My brother-in-law was head of purchasing for the company, and he always sent the lowest-priced ingredients to my plant. We also had

Frank's Story (continued)

a very clever accounting manager who could make our financial reports look good even when they weren't. As a result of all this, the Little Beaverton plant was able to cover up some, well, shall we say pressing productivity issues.

"Tony told me about all this and said that he had no intention of trying to embarrass me or the plant, but just wanted to do what was right for the company. Where do they get these guys?" Frank smirked.

Presumably what was right for the company in this case was to address the productivity issue head on. The cola company was large, and Tony pointed out other plants in the system probably faced similar problems and had found ways to overcome them. He suggested using the company's collective intelligence and experience to help bring the Little Beaverton plant's productivity up to standard. But that's not the way Frank saw it.

"Look, the meeting he held with me to talk about this stuff did not go well, not at all," Frank said. "I didn't deny any of what Tony said to me, but I clearly didn't want to talk about it. I spent most of the meeting just glaring at him, grinding my teeth. He just didn't get it and kept going on and on about how we could talk to other plants to figure out what they had done to improve their productivity. How would that make *me* look?

"I told him, 'Look, I know you want to make a big name for yourself back at headquarters, but I'm not the guy to trash to do it,' " Frank recounted, stabbing his finger at us, the same way I imagine he must have done to Tony. "Then he says to me, 'That's not what I'm trying to do here, Frank. Honestly, I just want to help. I just want to do the right thing.' Come on, who's this guy think he's fooling anyway?

"I told him, 'If you know what's good for you, you'll get the hell out of my office and forget all this crap. You haven't told me anything we didn't already know anyway. We've got plans to fix all that stuff. I don't have to answer to you as to how we're going to do it. We're through discussing this.' " Frank told us that at that point, he turned his back to Tony and stared out the office window.

Frank had always been uncomfortable with the plant's involvement with this START program, and now his every concern was proven valid. In Frank's mind, Tony was a corporate spy sent to find out everything the plant was doing wrong and report back on it. The more Frank thought about it, the more incensed he became.

"Just who the hell did this kid think he was, anyway?" Frank demanded. "Nobody in this plant would have even dared to speak to me the way that he did. They know they'd never live to tell about it. I wanted to show him that he couldn't challenge me like that."

The very next day Frank called up his boss and told him that Tony simply had to leave the plant. "I gave him the kiss of death. I said, 'Bill, look, I'm telling you he's just not a leader; he doesn't inspire any confidence. He's been a bull in a china shop since he got here, and he's really upset a lot of people.' "

Frank knew his words would seal the young executive's fate at this particular company. The company wanted "leaders who inspire confidence" in the executive ranks, and it was generally felt that leadership was innate—"either he's got it or he doesn't." Part of the company's promotion process was to weed out people who lacked this "natural" leadership quality. Frank knew he could be ruining Tony's career, but he was enraged enough not to care.

A few weeks later, a human resources executive visited the plant and fired Tony. He explained to Tony that he "had not succeeded in winning the confidence of the plant" and that he had no further assignment with the company.

"Look, I didn't like getting this guy fired, but there really wasn't any choice in the matter," Frank rationalized. "I had to protect my interests." Undoubtedly it will be a long time before Frank has to suffer another intrusion from the START program.

Let's take a closer look at the forces behind Frank's behavior.

TYPE OF POLITICAL BEHAVIOR: Working to fire an underling who is perceived as a threat.

IMPAIRMENT TO THE COMPANY: The loss of an executive's vital and effective analysis of a plant's productivity.

PERSONAL MOTIVATION: Anger, fear.

Frank's Story (continued)

CONTRIBUTING WEAK INSTITUTIONAL DYNAMICS: Deficiency of meaningful goals regarding performance, lack of accountability, absence of pay for performance, insularity.

EFFECT ON THE COMPANY'S PROFITS: Low productivity, high costs of manufacturing, loss of a well-trained and motivated executive.

DEBRIEFING

What went wrong here? To begin with, the plant manager was not rewarded based on his plant's productivity. Thus, he had no incentive to improve it. When a corporate executive uncovered the issue and offered his support to help improve productivity, the plant manager viewed his offer as nothing more than a challenge to his authority and position.

How do you think Frank would have reacted if he had had a 30 percent bonus riding on improving productivity? Chances are that he would have welcomed whatever insight and assistance the corporate executive could have offered.

Because Frank had no personal incentive to improve productivity, or indeed any other clear and measurable performance metric, he spent his energies building and securing his empire. He spent more time thinking about the power he had inside the plant than he did about doing his job and improving the plant's performance.

Another important point here is the performance evaluation process for Tony. His performance evaluation, like that of the plant manager, had nothing to do with meeting objective measurements. It all came down to the plant manager's call and his perceptions of Tony's "leadership capabilities" (however he personally defined them). Although Tony had invested a great deal of time determining the "right thing to do for the company," which its stockholders would appreciate, he personally would have been better off by not making any attempts to improve the plant's performance.

In both cases, weak institutional dynamics undermined real success. Specifically, the performance measures in this scenario were vague, not measurable, and not tied to making improvements. As we've seen, office politics thrive in this sort of environment.

Have you ever seen personal anger and animosity derail a career in your company?

CHAPTER 3

The Doctor Is In
Examining a Political Work Environment

The average business is a lot like Washington, D.C. Everybody knows there are common objectives somewhere. But the common objectives get lost in a cacophony of turf wars and special interest pleading. —JOHN CASE, *Open-Book Management*

R ecall for a moment your first week at the company or organization you work for now. You probably received from the human resources department some type of handbook or binder containing personnel polices. In a broad sense, it could be thought of as the "rule book." It might have even contained a section about the company's values that described a kind of code of conduct, or guidelines for how people should be treated in the company. In any case, it described how people were supposed to behave there.

If this job wasn't your first one out of school, you knew enough to smile and pay an appropriate amount of lip service to the HR rule book but not to take it too seriously. After all, that was only the official policy; you wanted to see the *real rules.*

The *Insider's Rule Book*

Now imagine that on your first day your boss handed you a hefty 200-page binder called the *Insider's Rule Book*.

This set of rules is the real deal. The *Insider's Rule Book* describes all that you need to know to fit right in and succeed—the *real* dos and don'ts of the company. In essence, this manual helps you understand what is in your own best interest and what the most likely consequences of your words or actions will be. Like economist Adam Smith's "invisible hand," it will guide all of your decisions.

That scenario would have been great, but in reality, chances are your company never a printed version of the *Insider's Rule Book*. But that doesn't mean the rule book doesn't exist, does it? Of course it exists; the trick is you've got to figure out the rules yourself over time.

Jack M., a vice president of sales and marketing for one of the largest consumer products companies in the United States, described to us some of the "pages" from the *Insider's Rule Book* at his company. You might recognize that some of these rules are operating in your company as well.

"No hard feelings here, these are just the rules of the company," Jack said. "Nobody talks about them, but we all play by them, and they're more important than anything we ever got from personnel.

"Okay, here goes. It works like this: Never admit a mistake; it will be used against you, probably indirectly but it will be used. Never discuss an issue without knowing where others stand first; you need to know who you're standing with and against. Never tell anyone anything that can be used against you, because, believe me, it will. Don't push for clarification or direction from your superiors, because, frankly, they probably don't know and you'll only make them feel uncomfortable—which is the last thing you want. Never help out anyone if it does not benefit your job. It'll never do you any real good; it just doesn't count. It's okay to betray a friend if it benefits your career; I've seen it happen all the time. Tell top executives what you think they want to hear, and just remember, intimidation works when all else fails."

Hold on here. Are people really that malleable? Do they actually adapt their behavior to a work environment? We might all work together in the same place, but we're still individuals, right?

Not as much as you'd think. At least a hundred different university studies have proven the point. I could cite well-known reports from Princeton, UCLA, or Wake Forest. But I think Alan Funt, the off-beat creator of television's classic *Candid Camera* proved the point as well as anyone. In one episode of the show that put unwitting subjects in extraordinary situations, a man enters an empty elevator. At the next floor, the elevator stops and another man walks in, presses a button, and then turns from the doors to face the back of the elevator. Weird, huh? At the next stop, another man enters and does exactly the same thing. After a third man enters and repeats the exercise, the first man, acting as if there was nothing at all unusual about all this behavior, casually turns around and faces the back of the elevator too.

That's the power of the *Insider's Rule Book*. An *Insider's Rule Book* at odds with established official policy or unclear rules only contributes to confusion and anxiety—two precursors of office politics.

Office Politics and Leadership

A clear and uncomplicated research project dating back to the fall of 1938 underscores this point.[1] Ronald Lippitt and Ralph White designed experiments with boys' clubs using such typical activities as arts and crafts. They set out to compare the effects of a democratic leadership style with an autocratic one, but an unplanned twist in the study revealed something far more interesting and completely unexpected.

When acting as authoritarian leaders during the first few sessions, Lippitt and White set the goals and performance criteria, gave instructions, made all the decisions, and criticized work. When Lippitt and White took on the role of democratic leaders during the next series of sessions, they guided the groups to establish goals and performance criteria and encouraged the boys to evaluate each other's work objectively.

No surprises here: Under democratic leadership the boys stuck to the tasks, were very friendly and cooperative, and achieved all of their goals. Under autocratic leadership, however, the boys lost interest in their task, fought, damaged materials, and showed no concern for the group's goals or each other's interests. So in attaining goals, democratic leadership beats authoritarian leadership (like I said, no surprises here).

Then Lippitt had another idea, and things got really interesting. In addition to testing the boys in autocratic and democratic environments, Lippitt and White tested them in an environment in which they offered no leadership. They gave the boys ambiguous goals, unclear performance criteria, unfocused instructions, and no predefined consequences. (Does this situation sound anything like where you work?)

The results under this laissez-faire arrangement were disastrous. The boys showed less task focus than under either of the other leadership styles. The lack of direction frustrated the boys, who felt inadequate and blamed their unhappiness on less able members. They accomplished considerably less than they had under the democratic or authoritarian leadership style.

Lippitt and White arrived at the same conclusion that every comparable study has repeated ever since: For people to work together effectively *proj.* and achieve high performance goals, people need a clear sense of what the *mgmt* objectives are, an explicit understanding of how they fit in, and unambiguous expectations of the rewards or consequences they face.

How would you describe the leadership style in your company? Is it democratic or authoritarian? It's most likely neither.

A Matter of Degree

Before getting into the diagnostics of this chapter, it's worthwhile answering a question that I often hear. People frequently ask, "How much office politics is too much?" What they are really asking is whether they can ignore their organizations' enemy within and accept it as just part of doing business. It is a legitimate question.

The answer, of course, is it depends. It depends on how much the political environment is undermining the organization's ability to do the following:

- To make good business decisions

- To attract and retain the best people

- To compete in the marketplace

We have found that the political environment undermines all of these aspects in concert; they interact and feed one another.

By the end of this chapter, with all of its diagnostic tools, you will be able to assess the degree to which office politics and the enemy within exist in your organization. Then you can see how much is too much for yourself.

Common Characteristics

How can you tell if you're in a political environment? James McTaggart, Peter Kontes, and Michael Mankins, the authors of *The Value Imperative,* answer the question this way:

> *The symptoms of this corporate disease are many, including . . . a focus primarily on internal rather than external performance requirements; a high tolerance for business units that consistently perform poorly; formulation of "strategic" rationales for obviously uneconomic acquisitions; build up of excessive overhead; an organization matrix that promotes unclear or multiple responsibilities for performance; incentive programs with generous payouts regardless of performance, and vacuous mission statements. All of these are symptoms of the institutional attempt to put economic sheep's clothing on the political wolf of the institutional imperative.[2] (Emphasis added.)*

Barbara Bailey Reinhold, the author of *Toxic Work,* uses more everyday language to describe a political workplace:

> *People . . . take credit for others' work and steal others' accounts, clients, and ideas. They also sabotage others, discriminate against people who are different from them, hurt others' feelings, discount others' achievements, and cause fights unnecessarily. It's also likely that someone . . . consistently doesn't deliver, and nothing happens to correct the situation. Lots of workplaces seem unsafe or out of control because of these . . . behaviors and situations.[3]*

Do either of these descriptions fit your organization?

Some other characteristics of political environments are more subtle and perhaps not quite so ubiquitous.

Politically Dominant Organizations Make Tacit, Rather Than Explicit, Decisions

This type of decision making avoids creating an "audit trail" for a decision and thus provides an out in case things don't work as planned. That way when someone asks, "Why didn't we match the competition's 10 percent cut in prices in the Northeast region?" workers can just shrug. "Well, let's see here, nobody can recall the fine points exactly, and no one explicitly said not to. I suppose it was just the general conclusion at the time."

Politically Dominant Organizations Are Crisis Oriented

Some people use the term *crisis culture* to describe this phenomenon. Here's the way it operates: While some type of planning process exists, the plan is unceremoniously scrapped with the glimmer of the first unforeseen event, which quickly takes on the form of a crisis. All bets are off. This changes everything. The payoffs for this behavior are a crisis gives people a sense of importance, and managers can use them as excuses for erratic action and for a failure to meet commitments.

The crisis culture tends to perpetuate itself. A crisis in one department impacts all the departments or areas it relates to, in turn affecting all the areas that those departments deal with and so on. It often goes full circle to the department with the original crisis. A crisis causes an effect like dropping a pebble in a pond and watching the ripples in the water collide with one another. In a crisis culture, however, it's actually like watching handfuls of pebbles tossed into a pond over and over again.

The crisis culture perpetuates itself in another important way: It takes on a glamour all its own so that operating in a crisis mode almost seems desirable. For example, groups operating in a crisis culture often demean others that are able to think ahead and execute their plans well. The latter group is derided for seemingly "having it easy" rather than recognized for their ability to anticipate events and plan effective responses.

While the crisis culture might infect any company, it appears disproportionately in political organizations. It provides a powerful mechanism to evade responsibility, which is our next topic.

Politically Dominant Organizations Evade Responsibility

First, people avoid committing to measurable results. One president of a consumer goods company would commit to "raising awareness of quality" but not actually to improving the quality of his product. Clever man.

If forced to make any commitments, people in political environments qualify them. For example: "Sure, I can raise sales by 10 percent next year just as long as I can hire twenty more salespeople, no new products hit the market, our competition doesn't pull any surprises, and customers' buying patterns don't change. Then it's possible, sure, but it's still going to be a stretch." Some commitment.

Finally, if they have been forced to make a commitment and for whatever reason they can't fulfill their promises, people in political organizations always have a good excuse. If they were smart and qualified their commitment to begin with, they have a built-in excuse. ("Hey, remember I said I could do it if I could hire enough salespeople? Well, guess what?") If not, they might find a timely crisis to blame.

Paradoxically, excuses are more frequent and more accepted in political organizations. While workers often perceive these environments as tough, what makes them demanding isn't an insistence on meeting measurable performance goals, it's having to battle with the enemy within. If you work the system well enough, play a good game, and line up the right support, however, your excuses for not meeting your goals won't be challenged.

There Are Many "Undiscussables" in Politically Dominant Organizations

Harvard educator Chris Argyris coined the term *undiscussable* in an article he wrote for the *Harvard Business Review* in 1986.[4] An undiscussable is *a known problem or issue that people in an organization will not talk about openly*. It is like having an elephant in the living room that everyone's trying to ignore. Everyone knows it's there because they have to walk around it, yet everyone refuses to acknowledge it. Nobody ever asks, "Hey, what are we going to do about this damn elephant in the living room?"

People are even reluctant to admit that an undiscussable is, in fact, undiscussable. Thus, an issue's undiscussability itself often becomes off-limits.

Although undiscussables are not talked about in open forums where they can be honestly examined and resolved, they do get airtime. They are whispered about in hallways and restrooms, discussed among close allies, and gossiped about by early arrivals at a meeting. They often become secrets everyone knows.

So what are some of the more common undiscussables? Frequently the list includes the performance of the company's senior management (especially if it's been poor), money-losing projects or divisions (especially if they have high-level sponsorship), company morale (especially if it's low), and office politics (favoritism, masterminding, character assassination, and so on).

The truly insidious aspect of undiscussables is that the issues they represent never improve. How can anyone resolve them if they aren't dealt with openly and honestly? Such undiscussables as office politics often remain unchecked and spread like a cancer, crippling an organization's effectiveness. To see if your company is at that point, invest some time in the diagnostic tests that follow.

Bear in mind that most of these tests are commonly administered to large numbers of people within an enterprise to obtain a representative cross section of perspectives. You should view your individual results, therefore, as a reflection of your personal experience in your immediate work group and functional area. They can provide a directional sense of the extent of office politics in your organization but not necessarily a definitive response.

Diagnostic Tests
Exercise 1. Symptoms of a Political Workplace

Here we've organized some specific characteristics of a political environment. These traits, some of which are subtle, have been collated from well over 100 case studies and company interviews. You simply need to write whether the following statements are true or false for your organization:

BHA   JA

___ Problems are never fully resolved.

___ Meetings end without making decisions (apart from further study).

___ Everyone knows who the scapegoats are.

___ There are "secrets" that everyone knows but do not openly discuss.

___ Directions from superiors are ambiguous.

___ Humor in the office is cynical or demeaning.

___ Excuses are accepted from powerful people.

___ Most people eat lunch at their desks.

___ Less powerful people are slighted, shunned, or otherwise marginalized for perceived failure.

___ Associating with slighted individuals can be cause for derision from coworkers.

___ Information is gated by departments and individuals.

___ Cooperation is given in direct proportion to the hierarchical position of the person asking for it.

___ People don't talk about their lives outside of the office.

___ There is a widespread use of outside consultants, especially in strategic planning.

___ Opinions from powerful people are treated as facts.

___ People make only qualified commitments from which they can easily backpedal.

___ Nobody can recite the company's goals.

___ People don't know how they directly contribute to the company's goals.

___ People attending a meeting do not speak up unless they are specifically asked for information.

Anyone working in an organization will agree with at least a few of these statements, but have you answered more than half of them with "true"? If so, you have the first signal that you are working in a politically dominant organization.

· ·
Exercise 2. Have You Ever. . . ?

This exercise asks whether you have ever been in a given situation in your present organization. Simply check the box if your answer is yes. Don't agonize over each answer; go with your first response. Have you ever:

B Hp   Jp

❑ Been told by your boss, however subtly, *not* to supply information to another group within the company?

❑ Seen a qualified coworker forced out of a job?

☒ Felt that people were being rewarded more for perceived effort than for actual results?

☒ Felt discomfort raising a legitimate business issue facing the company?

❑ Seen people adamantly believe in something, only to change their minds in a meeting when a key player disagreed?

☒ Seen a great idea die because of a lack of cooperation?

❑ Been told, however subtly, *not* to cooperate with someone?

☒ Felt that the best way to get ahead was not to upset anyone?

☒ Heard your management publicly say they value one thing, but their actions demonstrate they value something else?

❑ Seen that people who get upset get their way?

☒ Felt really confused about what you're supposed to be doing?

❑ Been asked to make an assessment of some aspect of the business and then been told by your boss, subtly or not, what exactly the assessment should conclude?

☒ Had reason to believe that performance reviews are based simply on whether the boss likes you?

☑ Felt that to get along you've got to go along?

☑ Seen people sit quietly through a meeting, then complain afterward about the decision that was made?

❑ Been mystified why someone left the company?

☑ Seen important business decisions made based on personalities instead of facts?

❑ Not been clear about your department's goals?

❑ Seen someone ambushed in a meeting?

❑ Not been able to find out who was responsible for something?

☑ Seen people stay late just to prove their commitment?

How many checks do you have? A simple majority is your second signal that you are working in a politically dominant organization.

•
Exercise 3. How Attractive Is Your Company?

A little-known research project at the University of Chicago collected an astounding 17 million surveys of workers in some forty countries around the world. The survey was intended to determine what people really needed from their workplace to be able to operate at their peak performance.

Eight consistent themes emerged from the surveys, underscoring the universal nature of what people really need to be successful in their work lives.[5] They reveal what makes an attractive and compelling work environment. All of these themes are completely incompatible with a political workplace.

Compiled below are the eight themes. Read each theme and think about the current situation in your organization. If you think your organization currently epitomizes this theme, give it a ten. On the other hand, if you think your organization is completely lacking in this area, give it a zero. Most likely you'll score each theme somewhere in between.

<u>J</u> Truth

<u>F</u> Trust

<u>F</u> Honesty

<u>F</u> Openness

<u>T</u> Caring

<u>T</u> Giving credit

<u>T</u> Mentoring

<u>F</u> Risk taking

Now comes the fun part. We have placed the eight themes around the wheel in figure 3-1. Zero represents the center of the circle, and a ten represents the perimeter. Take your scores and mark the appropriate place for each theme with a dot. Next, connect all the dots with a line. Examine the gap between the perimeter of the circle and the line you've just drawn. This gap represents the difference be-

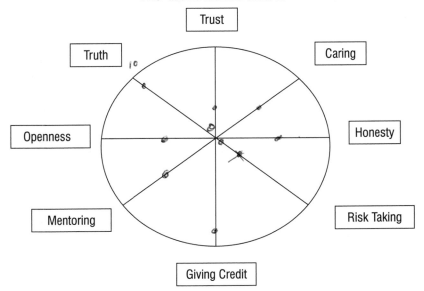

FIGURE 3-1
The Work Ideals Wheel

tween the ideal work environment and what you are living in now, which is affected by the enemy within your organization.

Figure 3-2 is an example of a completed chart, just to give you a sense of what yours might look like.

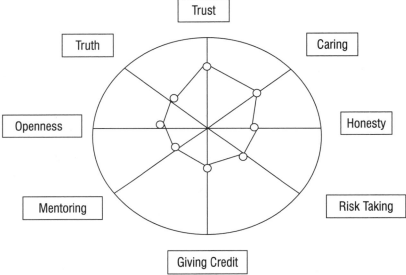

FIGURE 3-2
A Sample Work Ideals Wheel

Trust

Truth

Caring

Openness

Honesty

Mentoring

Risk Taking

Giving Credit

Exercise 4. Write It Down

For this next exercise, you will become an author. This straightforward activity requires only that you be honest with yourself. Pull out a pen and a single sheet of paper.

Using just a few sentences, write down a meaningful work problem you've been chewing on. Estimate the cost of the problem in dollars, downtime, efficiency, customer goodwill, or whatever measure is appropriate. Next, write down what you think is the right solution to this problem, keeping it to a few sentences. Then estimate the benefits. Next, write down the name of the person you think would be most resistant to this solution. Now you're ready to "talk" to him.

Take out another sheet of paper, and draw a line down the middle of the page. Using the left-hand side, write down what you'd say to that person about your problem and solution. Using the right-hand column, write what you think his reply and his feelings—threatened, empowered, bored, and so forth—about your proposal would be. Now write your reply on the left-hand side of the page. Repeat this process until you've reached a conclusion or dead end.

Now go back and examine what you wrote. What is the nature of his objections? Are you being asked to supply more information, facts, and analysis? If so, that's fair; you need to get the data and approach him again. Take this exercise as one indication that your organization might not be overrun with the enemy within and that your company places more emphasis on analysis than politics.

On the other hand, perhaps the argument is not about facts and analysis. Does he simply stonewall you and refuse to discuss your proposal? Does he try to obscure the issue or otherwise evade it? Does he hide behind another decision that's already been made that he claims addresses your issue? Does he invoke some powerful person's name or otherwise try to intimidate you? In this case, then, investigation, fact gathering, and analysis won't do you much good. You have a political fight on your hands. Take this exercise as a meeting with the enemy within and as a window on the way tough issues are handled in your company.

In your writing, you have tapped into all the subtle cues from your work environment and all the lessons you've learned about how people work with each other and deal with conflict in your company. Perhaps even unknowingly you have amassed a composite view of the political realities and the enemy within your organization, and they are displayed before you.

Exercise 5. Language Lessons

Below is a list of brief statements that are used, not so subtly, to intimidate others and create self-doubt. In our research, these statements are used with much greater frequency in highly political organizations than in companies that have worked to eliminate the enemy within and to develop a safe work environment. Check each statement you've heard in the past month, whether it was used on you or someone else:[6]

❑ You're going to say/write/do *that*?

❑ Don't even think about it!

❑ Why do you feel *that* way?

❑ You're slow/crazy/dumb/clumsy/always/never—!

❑ Why can't you be more like me/him/her?

❑ Come on, now. You *can't* be angry/disappointed/frustrated/annoyed.

❑ You aren't going to work on *that* project, are you?

To evaluate your test, count your check marks, and record the result. If more than three of these expressions have been used in your presence in the past month, then you've experienced intimidation and other forms of control that are indicative of a politically dominated workplace.

Exercise 6. How True Is This for You?

This exercise is quick and personal. All you need to do is think about yourself in your work environment and state whether you agree or disagree with the following statements:

_____ I can be myself.

_____ I can speak plainly, without mincing words.

_____ I trust my boss.

_____ I trust my coworkers.

_____ People share information with me freely.

_____ People cooperate with me.

_____ I can rely on my coworkers.

_____ My coworkers can rely on me.

_____ I feel accountable for specific results.

_____ I feel respected by my colleagues.

_____ My boss lets me know I'm appreciated.

_____ I have no doubt that my hard work will pay off in a high performance rating.

If you predominantly disagree, this is the final indication that you work in a politically dominant organization. Consider the implications before proceeding to the final exercise.

· ·
Exercise 7. Pulling It All Together

All of the exercises in this chapter work to capture the nature of your work environment and to test for signs of the enemy within. You have looked at your organization through the lens of a political work environment, and now you can see for yourself how closely your company fits this picture.

You can summarize all that you have learned by assessing three final statements. They represent the fundamental core of what we have been exploring in the previous diagnostics. Thus, review your previous work, and reflect on your findings. Then sharpen that pencil one more time, and answer whether you agree or disagree with the following three statements about your organization:

_____ People don't feel safe.

_____ People are not rewarded based on merit.

_____ People who play by the rules don't win after all.

These three statements are at the heart of our definition of a political work environment and the enemy within. You could have jumped ahead to this final exercise (and shame on you if you did), but by completing the other diagnostics first, this last exercise is more meaningful. Your sense of conviction is greatly increased.

So if your suspicions about whether your organization is harboring the enemy within have been confirmed, that, of course, begs the question, What can you do about it? We'll cover that topic in part II.

Notes

1   Marvin Weisbord, *Productive Workplaces: Organizing for Dignity, Meaning, and Community* (San Francisco: Jossey-Bass, 1987), 82–84.

2   James McTaggart, Peter Kontes, and Michael Mankins, *The Value Imperative* (New York: The Free Press, 1994), 46.

3   Barbara Bailey Reinhold, *Toxic Work: How to Overcome Stress, Overload, and Burnout and Revitalize Your Career* (New York: Dutton Books, 1996), 77.

4   Christopher Argyris, "Skilled Incompetence," *Harvard Business Review* (September–October 1986), 77.

5   Rob Lebow and William L. Simon, *Lasting Change: The Shared Values That Make a Company Great* (New York: Van Nostrand Reinhold, 1997), preface.

6   John Freil and Linda Freil, *An Adult Child's Guide to What Normal Is* (Deerfield Beach, Fla.: Health Communications, 1990), 133–34.

Brent's Story

CASE STUDY: A manager is afraid to make a recommendation that would save the company millions of dollars, because it reflects poorly on a previous decision made by the company's president.

POLITICAL RESPONSE: The manager buries the recommendation.

This story represents another sort of office politics, one that harms the shareholders. This situation is nearly ubiquitous in corporate life.

Meet Brent T., a twenty-year veteran of Consolidated Technologies, a large conglomerate of electronics companies. As a research manager, Brent gets involved with special project work, analyzing different markets and areas of the business. Here's his story.

"Occasionally I get a hot potato dropped in my lap—you know, an assignment with the potential for a 'career-limiting' move, like forcing a recommendation that could land me in hot water with some of the higher-ups."

Brent explained, "What's saved me is that I've got a pretty good sense for these things, and I've never gotten anyone's nose out of whack. Believe me, the bosses I've had have always seemed pretty appreciative. You should see how dumb some other guys have been, not knowing when *not* to tell the truth."

When we spoke to Brent, he had just recently wrapped up an assignment he jokingly referred to as "the mother of all hot potatoes." It involved the potentially lethal combination of a poorly selling product and the company's president.

"You want to hear a good one?" Brent asked. "We make these Game Boy knockoffs that have never sold well. The plant that makes them is operating at only 40 percent of its capacity, and that's just about unheard of. The typical plant in their system operates at somewhere between 75 percent on the low end to 98 percent of capacity on the upper end. I knew that inventory levels in the plant were bulging, but I was shocked to hear just how bad the situation was when my boss told me."

His boss also explained that that morning the U.S. director of oper-

Brent's Story (continued)

ations had called, asking his group to analyze whether the plant should remain open or be shut down and outsource production to Taiwan. Normally a report like this one would be a no-brainer. After all, operating at a mere 40 percent of capacity drives production costs unbearably high and reduces profit margins to untenable levels. But there was a reason why this decision was more complicated than it first appeared.

"The problem was that our company's president, Mr. Wilson, for a time ran the new product development area of the company, where he pioneered the strategy of creating products for children to establish them as lifelong customers," Brent explained. "One of the first products that Consolidated Technologies developed under his strategy was this shameful knockoff of Nintendo's Game Boy. It came in assorted colors, or 'flavors' as the ads said, and matched nearly every feature of its rival's. It kind of became a symbol for the new strategy and new direction for the company."

According to Brent, first-year sales had been somewhat promising, and a new plant was commissioned to manufacture the product. This cost was justified by the forecasts of astonishing sales growth—more than 80 percent a year for the first five years out, trailing off to a more modest 35 percent growth thereafter. (How those projections were developed, and under what circumstances, could make for another illustration of office politics.)

"From what I hear, even as the plant was under construction, sales began to trail off, but building continued under the assumption that sales would spring back. The plant was completed, and in the dedication ceremony, the then-president of the company apparently said, 'It's a good thing we kept the blueprints for this plant, because if sales go as planned, we're going to be needing another one soon!' "

Brent told us that unfortunately sales did not go as well as planned, and much of the plant remained idle. Yet management talked about the product like it was a success, and every headquarters employee had one at home (although some employees bought their children the more popular and reliable Game Boy as well). The sales figures were never circulated, so not many people knew about the product's actual lackluster performance. Even fewer people realized that because it was carrying the expense of a dedicated plant, it was being manufactured for twice the cost of its competitor.

"So think about what I was being told to do," Brent said. "Unless the projected future sales could justify it, the plant would be shut down and manufacturing outsourced somewhere else. This would all make good economic sense. But it would highlight that the product did not turn out to be the success people had once thought it would be. How would Mr. Wilson, the product's developer and now president, react to that?

"I could either tell the truth, which was that there was no way the sales of that product would ever justify keeping the plant open, and risk embarrassing Mr. Wilson," Brent told us, "or come up with some way to say, 'Keep her open.' Believe me, if you've been here long enough, you'd know there's a downside risk of making one of the higher-ups look bad and not a lot of risk in keeping their reputations intact. Got it?"

We learned from Brent that anybody analyzing market and sales trends for the product would have been hard-pressed to justify keeping an entire plant dedicated to it. Outsourcing the manufacturing to Taiwan would have saved the company $1.5 million a year, and the company could have netted an estimated $4 million by selling the existing facility. The decision, based on pure economics and in the best interests of the shareholders, should have been an easy one to make.

But recommending that action could be career limiting, as Brent was well aware. What he needed to do instead was to find some rationale, some special angle, some way to justify an inherently unjustifiable expense. Fortunately for Brent, he had encountered similar circumstances before.

"The first thing I did," Brent recalled, "was go to the marketing department and ask about their future plans for the product and their read on the market. They weren't that helpful. Nobody was excited about the product or the future of the market. There were many other products with much higher potential, and that's what they were focusing on."

However, in his own research, Brent found out about an emerging

Brent's Story (continued)

technology that could enable players to download games from the Internet onto handheld devises like the Game Boy knockoff. This idea was just the ticket that he had been looking for.

He admitted, "Sure, it was flimsy, almost to the point of being laughable, and I certainly didn't believe in it myself. But that wasn't the point. It provided me with the rationale, however slim, for projecting a turnaround in sales."

He assembled a small team from his research department to build a business plan based on the promise of this new technology and on what he called "rather heroic assumptions" about future sales.

"In the final presentation, I stressed the need to think strategically and not be shortsighted and miss the Internet's tidal wave of change." Brent smiled, seeming to recall the moment. "They *loved* it, just ate it up. Of course, the plant would stay open with the colossal potential for future sales.

"The thing is my job was safe. It wasn't my decision to make—to keep the plant open or not. It was just my job to analyze whether future sales might support it." Brent paused before completing his thought. "Actually, if you want to know what my *real* job was, it was making our president look good. And that wouldn't have happened if I told the truth now, would it?"

Let's take a closer look at Brent's story.

TYPE OF POLITICAL BEHAVIOR: Misrepresenting the truth to avoid potential political fallout.

IMPAIRMENT TO THE COMPANY: Management's ability to make business decisions based on effective, factual analysis.

PERSONAL MOTIVATION: Fear.

CONTRIBUTING WEAK INSTITUTIONAL DYNAMICS: Lack of accountability for financial performance, insularity.

EFFECT ON THE COMPANY'S PROFITS: Unneeded expense of $1.5 million a year for the foreseeable future.

DEBRIEFING

The institutional dynamics that govern individual self-interest at Consolidated Technologies—the *Insider's Rule Book* that lets people know what the likely consequences of their actions will be—told Brent he had better come up with the politically correct answer regarding the plant. He saw no incentive to give the right answer, the answer that was in the best interests of the company and its stockholders.

But what happened in this case is repeated nearly every day across corporate America. An underling is asked to perform an analysis and make a recommendation, but after an objective examination of the facts, he or she finds a "politically unacceptable" answer.

Younger employees tend to be a bit slower in putting aside the right answer for the one that is more politically acceptable. More idealistic, they tend to want to tell the truth and do the right thing, while more seasoned, battle-scarred veterans find it's not always worth the fight.

The ones that suffer are the company and its stockholders, who, in this case, watch their shareholder value diminish by $1.5 million a year because a business decision was based on politics rather than analysis. The word *watch* here isn't entirely accurate; it's not as if the shareholders can watch the company as it make its decisions. If they did, then who would be willing to explain to them why the company was spending an extra $1.5 million a year unnecessarily just to keep from jeopardizing the president's ego?

The company suffers yet another cost, but it is more difficult to quantify. A company reaps valuable talent when it allows an employee like Brent to develop and hone his analytical skills over time. It means he can offer more insight, more valuable analysis, and simply better decision making. Yet when an employee like Brent operates in a political environment, the skills he learns are how to twist and manipulate data to support political decisions. This scheming is often referred to as "using smoke and mirrors." While this skill might be helpful to individuals who seek such support, it is detrimental to the company's shareholders. Ultimately, it also undermines the employee's confidence in his own analytical skills, because they are not really put to use.

Have you ever seen someone bury the truth in your company?

CHAPTER 4

The Zucchini of Questionable Freshness
Self-Interest, Politics,
and the *Insider's Rule Book*

*The important point for any management is that office politics
should never be tolerated because it is a form of self-aggrandize-
ment which, if not curbed, will destroy the morale of and forward
thrust of any organization.*
   —HAROLD GENEEN (CEO, ITT, 1959–1977)

Institutional dynamics can foster sound decision making or a political
environment, depending on the nature of the company. Such popular
programs as reengineering and other worthwhile initiatives will "stick"
only if they are introduced in a favorable environment, where the *Insider's
Rule Book* encourages people to do the right thing. If the *Insider's Rule
Book* does lead people to act in the best interest of the organization, then
management might not need to use these formalized corporate initiatives
again.

The following is an illustration that will demonstrate institutional dynamics and its role as an invisible hand in guiding people's behavior.

Think of this particular example as a small-scale model. With one quick glance, you can visualize the much larger issue it represents. Let's now revisit our friends at Microsoft and see how they managed to improve one rather burdensome process by changing the section in their *Insider's Rule Book* that governed the self-interests of a group of programmers.

Self-Interest and the Daily Build

One of the dullest tasks at Microsoft, or any software company for that matter, is doing something called "the daily build." For a long time, this task was assigned to an entry-level person at Microsoft and was widely considered to be grunt work. Here's why.

The daily build requires someone to take the code that many different programmers have written and piece it all together on one computer. The point is to ensure all of these pieces work separately and then together. The system breaks down if somebody's code isn't right, and the person doing the daily build needs to track the cause and get the right programmer to correct it.

As you can imagine, the daily build creates tension and a certain sense of "us versus them." Not surprisingly, the person assigned to the task of the daily build isn't exactly welcomed with opened arms. At Microsoft, for instance, they were thought of as "the code police," and the programmers gave them a hard time. (*Note:* If you ever want to be unpopular, volunteer to point out other people's errors, and, oh yeah, make sure these people are all senior to you.)

So here's a quick summary of the problem:

- The task of doing the daily build is "annoying but necessary."

- It is a costly process, even with junior people assigned to the task.

- It causes a great deal of friction between work groups. Programmers blame the "code police" for pestering them about coding errors, while the underlings doing the task blame the programmers for making their work harder.

- At the moment, it looks like little can be done about the matter; it's just the way it is.

In an average company, this situation might have gone on forever. Sure, the daily build is an inefficient process that sucks up time and creates bottlenecks, but what else can be done?

In a more ambitious company, perhaps somebody might have tried to reengineer the process or built a quality circle to address it. They might have reassessed the work flow and tried to come up with a more efficient process. But no matter how the work was redesigned, programmers would continue to make errors, and the "grunts" assigned to the daily build would still need to track and correct them. The programmers would still see the entire process as little more than a necessary evil and give it their minimal cooperation. Nothing would fundamentally change.

A manager at Microsoft, let's call her Kathy B., with a keen eye and plenty of imagination, saw a completely different approach to the problem. She changed the *Insider's Rule Book* that governed the programmers' self-interests.

Kathy realized that the people responsible for creating the errors, the programmers, were not held accountable for discovering or correcting those errors. The programmers then had little self-interest in the daily build, which was the root of the problem. Kathy changed the situation by changing the rules of the daily build. Here's what she proposed:

Rule 1. The daily build task will be performed by a full-fledged programmer, *not* by an underling.

Rule 2. That programmer will continue to be responsible for the daily build until someone hands him or her bad code.

Rule 3. The culprit handing in the bad code will become responsible for the daily build until someone hands him or her bad code.

Eventually, Kathy reasoned, every person would mess up. Each would have to take a turn as "the buildmeister."

With this new approach, the programmers' self-interests—and their behavior—changed literally overnight. Nobody wanted to be the buildmeister, so the programmers had a new, personal incentive to hand in error-free code. Beyond that, more experienced people now had a personal interest in attacking the problem, too. They wanted to minimize the time they spent on the daily build, so when their turn came, these talented people thought of new, effective ways to make corrections swiftly.

The programmers, being a spirited group, injected humor into their newfound responsibility. They wanted a symbol to show the passing of the baton from one buildmeister to another, but no traditional symbol would do for this irreverent lot. On a lark, someone brought in a giant zucchini, which was quickly anointed "the Zucchini of Questionable Freshness" and presented to the then-current buildmeister. Later, someone added a fake nose and glasses. A zucchini was passed on to a whole succession of buildmeisters.[1]

The result of all this cooperation (apart from injecting a sense of fun into arduous work) was quite remarkable. The number of errors plummeted, and the time spent on the daily build was drastically cut.

Note that the programmers accomplished this feat without any additional expense. In fact, expenses were actually reduced when the lower-level employees previously doing the daily build were reassigned. Also note Microsoft accomplished this transition without resorting to traditional redesign tools, such as fishbone diagrams, Pareto charts, or process flow mapping.

Kathy's approach had a completely different impact than the old rules, which merely led to underlings pleading with programmers, "Please cooperate with me." Looking at it from a higher vantage point, people's personal interests became aligned with a departmental goal, and the people who were the cause of a problem became accountable for fixing it. *In short, the rules of the work changed, not the work itself.*

In retrospect, Kathy's solution was the only workable answer. But if the resolution to the daily build problem now appears so clear, why wouldn't every company facing a similar problem arrive at the same solution? To answer that question, we'll need to look at the larger *Insider's Rule Book* at work in an average company and see why the workers would thwart this type of innovation.

While someone in an average company might also think of the same solution for the daily build problem, she might be reluctant to present it. The *Insider's Rule Book* would tell her that it's not worth running the risk of annoying the company's programmers and gaining another enemy within (especially when it's perfectly acceptable simply to continue to hire grunts for the work). Even if she had powerful convictions and presented this solution anyway, all it would take is one "You've *got* to be kidding" from the programmers—a powerful constituency in any software company—for management to kill her idea.

As we've seen, though, the *Insider's Rule Book* that governs Microsoft is different. Recall that what is at the heart of the company, or the essence of its corporate personality, is a drive to do what's best for the business. This idea was and is behind the thousands of decisions people make in the Microsoft enterprise every day.

The Microsoft programmers were therefore willing to try their manager's new idea, even if it meant taking on additional responsibility. They soon realized that it made sense for the same people who made the errors to be responsible for correcting them; it was the best business solution.

This simple example shows the power of addressing the *Insider's Rule Book* to improve performance. It also introduces a basic tenet of rewriting the *Insider's Rule Book* to eradicate political behavior: *Align personal interests with corporate interests.* In a political organization, this partnership is precisely what's lacking, which is a key reason why the enemy within is allowed to flourish there.

But making changes to the *Insider's Rule Book,* changes that can transform an organization once characterized by infighting and masterminding to one characterized by a collective sense of purpose, is clearly a significant undertaking. We'll explore the foundations of our team-based strategy to achieve that end in the next chapter.

Notes

1   Julie Bick, *All I Ever Need to Know in Business I Learned at Microsoft* (New York: Pocket Books, 1997), 19.

Tamara's Story

CASE STUDY: A marketing analyst is concerned that she's not quite up to leading a project, within her job description, that she's been assigned.

POLITICAL RESPONSE: She befriends the boss and compels him to make a less popular coworker accountable.

Of all the personal stories in this book, Tamara's is perhaps the easiest to relate to. We have all felt overwhelmed at one point or another, when we doubted that we could deliver what our bosses wanted. What option do we have other than to try our best and call for support when it's needed? Well, here's a costly alternative that one person used.

Tamara G. is a marketing analyst on the fund-raising side for a well-known not-for-profit organization. She spent nearly ten years working inside some of the largest consumer goods companies in the United States before deciding to "dial it down" and find a job in a less intense work environment.

"A couple of things surprised me about working here," Tamara confided. "The first is that, yes, it's a slower pace than what I was used to, but not as slow as I thought. There are still deadlines, revenue numbers to hit, even 'share' targets.

"The other thing that surprised me was that people here can be pretty naïve, very trusting. At my old company, you had to be politically savvy, or they'd eat you alive and sell the bones, but here, well, let's just say they're uninitiated for the most part. And, look, that's a good thing. Don't get me wrong—I love that. It's one of the reasons why I came here. I wanted to get away from all that.

"It's just that sometimes it can come in handy, you know, to have a few tricks up your sleeve that nobody's seen before. It has certain advantages."

Those "tricks" came in handy when Tamara was confronted with a major new project that she was expected to lead.

Her organization, let's call it Children in Need, had invested a sizable amount of its capital budget in a new computer system. It held a

Tamara's Story (continued)

repository of data on personal giving and contained a record of how much each individual donor gave, when, and under what specific appeal. The concept that originally sold Children in Need on the whole system was that the people on the fund-raising side could "mine" the data and develop more targeted appeals intended to attract specific types of donors. Rather than send twelve pieces of mail with different types of promotional literature in a year to a single address, a donor would instead receive just two pieces of mail with the type of appeal known to work best with him or her.

It took more than a year to get the computer systems converted, but at last the system was on-line and ready to be mined. The only problem was nobody knew much about mining data. They did have a sense, however, of the type of report they wanted to generate. That's where Tamara's expertise was supposed to come in.

"I kind of oversold myself on this aspect of the job," she confessed. "When Jeff, my boss, was interviewing me, he asked if I knew much about database systems and reporting. I told him that I did, and that, in fact, I had worked on a major computer conversion project that took almost two years and $40 million to complete. That was all true, but I was just a part-time member of a project team with close to fifty other people in it, and frankly, the outside consultants did most of the work.

"Jeff didn't seem to care that much about it. He did tell me that creating marketing reports, studies, and analysis from the new computer system was going to be part of my new job, but he downplayed it. So I thought, *Big deal, you know, with the advancements in computers these days they nearly do your thinking for you anyway, right? So what's to know?*"

Just four months into her new job, Jeff told her she needed to meet with the marketing managers and discuss what they wanted from the new system. Then she had to figure out how to get the information.

"I acted like it wasn't a big deal, but inside I felt my blood run cold," said Tamara, shaking her head as she recalled the moment. "What Jeff wanted me to do was really the hands-on work, getting in there and developing and running reports. I had never done anything like that before. I always had these tech support guys who would do that stuff.

"The first thing I did was go back to my job description, and sure enough, right there in black and white it says I'm supposed to head up this project to utilize the data-mining capability of the new system. I mean, there was no way out of it. I thought I'd just have to fess up that I couldn't do it and hope for the best."

But Tamara didn't give up quite that quickly.

"Then I thought about Susan, my colleague, who also reported to Jeff. She's this really bright, energetic person who always has a smile on her face. She's responsible for coordinating the different appeals programs, you know, making sure that everything happens when it's supposed to.

"Susan is one of those nice people types. You know, you give her a lot to do, and she just says, 'Jeez, I hope I can get it all done.' I'm not saying that people take advantage of her, but she doesn't exactly stick up for herself. Not the way I would. I mean, I wouldn't hesitate to tell someone to go to hell.

"So I thought, *Maybe I could pass this on to her.* The only problem was that nowhere in her job description did it mention anything about systems programming, building databases, or creating marketing re-ports—all the stuff that was in my job description. Her job was purely operational. I really thought I was stuck, especially because she's the only other person in the department. If I wanted to fob this off on someone else, I'd have to look outside the department, and that's al-ways a lot harder to do.

"But one thing I knew for certain was that Jeff really liked me. We played on the Children in Need softball team every Thursday in the summer, and we usually went out with the crew for pizza and beer afterward. We got along great. Whenever somebody would bust on Jeff, I'd bust that person right back. He loved it, I could tell. I was his little pit bull. He thought I was loyal, because I'd stick up for him.

"But Susan, on the other hand, never went out with us. She was newly married and liked to go home after work. That's great, I guess, but you can't win allies at work if you're at home, can you? She was at a disadvantage, and she didn't even know it. Sure, every once in a while

I'd see her face fall when Jeff and I shared an inside joke in front of her, but I don't think she ever fully understood she was the odd one out. Sure, we're all part of the team. It's just that, well, some of us are more equal than others," Tamara laughed.

Tamara devised a plan to put Susan in charge of the project. It wouldn't be easy, however; she'd need to give Jeff some reason for putting someone else in charge of her project. Tamara at least had to appear to be fair. "I call it my 'slide it on in' strategy," Tamara explained. "You just don't walk up to your boss and say, 'Give my co-worker my work, please.' You've got to ease into it. So I went to Jeff and told him I'd like Susan to work with me on the project, that I thought she could learn something valuable. We'd also gain some coverage in the department in case I was ever out for a period, and this way we'd be certain of coordinating our departmental efforts better in the future.

"It hit all of his hot buttons. He said he'd have to think about it, but I could tell from his smile that he'd agree to it. Basically, I gave him all the rationale he'd need if anyone ever questioned him on it. At our little staff meeting that Friday, he brought it up, and you should have seen Susan's face. It was all like, 'Huh?'

"Susan's the classic team player. Of course, she didn't object to it, but she wondered out loud how she was going to get it all done since her plate was already full. And I remember thinking, *You haven't seen the half of it.*"

Tamara's goal was not just to get Susan involved, but to transfer responsibility for the project. Tamara took it one step at a time. Once Susan had become a regular at the weekly meetings and started to make a contribution, Tamara seized another opportunity.

"I told Jeff that Susan really seemed enthusiastic, and that the other members of the team really seemed to like her, even look up to her," Tamara reported. "One of the biggest pieces of the project was to find out what exactly the marketing managers wanted out of the new system, what type of information and reports they wanted to see. I told Jeff that I thought Susan should spearhead that.

"I told him that Susan just seemed to speak their language and that maybe because I had come from industry that I just couldn't make the connection as quickly. I told him I was still learning and that for the good of the project Susan should take responsibility for what we called 'defining the requirements' of the new system.

"I earned points by looking humble, putting the good of the project in front of my own feelings, and simultaneously elevating a colleague," Tamara explained with a grin. "I mean, it was perfect. Jeff bought every word of it. Maybe it was because he simply wanted to, or because he was naïve, I don't know. But in any case, he agreed. I think Susan was a little pissed and maybe caught on to what I was doing at that point, because she stopped smiling at me. But that freight train had already left the station, and there was nothing she could do about it.

"Here's the thing. Doing the requirements definition is a huge piece of a project like that. Not only is it a lot of work, but nobody is in a position to know more about what the users want out of the system than the person who did the requirements definition. And the person who knows what the users want is the one who should provide it to them. Get the picture? So before Susan could do anything about it, she owned the project. It was hers.

"Suddenly I became the one just sitting at the conference table while Susan ran the meeting. Then scheduling conflicts would come up, and I had to miss a meeting, then another. Pretty soon, I had pretty well bowed out altogether."

Although no official announcement was ever made, unofficially Susan was recognized as the leader of the project. Meanwhile, Tamara faded out of the effort.

"It was a riot," Tamara told us. "Less than a year later Susan wound up leaving Children in Need, and Jeff officially rewrote her job description to include responsibility for data mining. Then get this: Two months after Susan left, I took a job over in special events. Jeff had nobody left in his department, because he couldn't get anyone to fill Susan's old job. So he rewrote the job descriptions, again, back to what they had been before I got there. Can you believe that?

"Funny how much just one person can influence things."

Tamara's Story (continued)

Let's look at Tamara's behavior more closely.

TYPE OF POLITICAL BEHAVIOR: Favoritism, transferring accountability and responsibility to another party.

IMPAIRMENT TO THE COMPANY: Deterioration in morale, with an already overtaxed coworker unable to tend to her official responsibilities effectively; misuse of scarce resources.

PERSONAL MOTIVATION: Fear, laziness.

CONTRIBUTING WEAK INSTITUTIONAL DYNAMICS: Lack of accountability, pay for performance, performance judged by goal achievement, and formal processes to review changes in job responsibilities.

EFFECT ON THE COMPANY'S PROFITS: No value from one coworker; additional recruiting and training expenses, loss of productivity, and brain drain.

DEBRIEFING

On the one hand, you can look at this situation as resulting from poor management. Jeff didn't treat one employee fairly, while he bent over backward for another. Eventually it cost him one hard-working employee and perhaps more than that if nobody else in the organization wanted to work for him. But that's his loss, and he will have to deal with it, right?

Not exactly. The institution incurs a cost as well. Nothing in an organization can ever stand completely on its own; everything is connected.

There's an obvious reason why Jeff found it impossible to hire anyone within the organization to replace Susan. People without a vested interest can usually spot what's fair and what's not pretty quickly. In this case, Susan's coworkers could obviously see that what was happening to her was unfair. The whole affair smacked of masterminding and political maneuvering, and it was clearly not in the best interest of Children in Need. The resulting detrimental impact on morale reverberated throughout the organization. In addition, people surely began to wonder if what happened in Jeff's area could happen in theirs.

Children in Need also wound up losing a valuable resource in Susan. Hard working, smart, knowledgeable, well liked, and dedicated—that's just the type of person you want to keep and want other workers to emulate. And when good people leave, others tend to follow.

So what happened? Tamara's motivation was pretty clear, and yes, Jeff was a weak manager. But what about the *Insider's Rule Book* allowed this situation to happen?

In an experiment conducted a few years ago, researchers asked participants to listen to a man being interviewed and to judge whether he was telling the truth. They gave the participants a remote control that would send a shock to the interviewee if for whatever reason they felt that he lied during the interview. Based on the level of lying that they perceived, the participants could shock the interviewee with different voltages. The remote had three settings—one for an insignificant lie, one for a material lie, and one for major deceit—with the last labeled as "extremely painful."

In actuality, the researchers used an actor for the interviewee. He could see in a hidden monitor the level of shock he had just received, and he'd act accordingly.

First, the participants sat in the same room as the interviewee, about fifteen feet away. In this setting, they administered fairly moderate "shocks," with almost no extremely painful shocks given. When the researchers moved the participants to an adjoining room with a two-way mirror, where they could observe a second new interviewee but he could not see them, the average shock administered quadrupled. They also chose an "extremely painful" shock a full third of the time. What a difference a little isolation makes.

Going back to Tamara's case, Jeff was safely isolated. He did what he pleased in terms of shifting job responsibilities, even to the point where he buried one of his employees with work by giving her a project that was in another employee's job description. The *Insider's Rule Book* at Children in Need told Jeff that he could do what he wanted in this regard. He could hit the "extremely painful" buzzer at will. Sure, he

Tamara's Story (continued)

might run the risk of losing a good employee, but that was his risk to take.

Furthermore, if Susan kicked up a fuss, she'd be in jeopardy of being labeled as "uncommitted" or "not a team player." She could do little but grin and bear it (while looking for another job).

While this type of situation might sound all too familiar to you, it certainly needn't be that way. Consider what might have happened here if the rules had been different. Say, for example, that all employees had to complete a simple "goal sheet," the type used at companies like American Express. (We'll describe this concept in detail in chapter 9.) A goal sheet is *a document that lays out an individual's goals for the upcoming year, how success will be measured, an overview of the plan to accomplish it, and so on.* It is reviewed and approved by that individual's manager, as well as the manager's boss, to ensure proper coordination and fairness. A copy of the goal sheet remains on file in the HR department, which facilitates and administers the process.

In this scenario, Tamara's attempt at a mid-year change in responsibilities and goals couldn't happen unless Jeff's boss reviewed and approved it, with the goal sheet formally amended and resubmitted to HR (for a sanity check). A boss like Jeff could try to "hide" the change by forcing it and telling Susan to keep quiet but only at great risk both to himself and to his boss, who would be held responsible for Jeff's managerial actions. In Tamara's situation, it would have been impossible to conceal the change anyway, because the highly visible project had many other people on the project team who would have noticed Tamara was no longer leading the project.

This type of rule change, altering the *Insider's Rule Book,* would remove the one-way mirror that Jeff previously hid behind. It would put him, along with his boss and HR, back in the room with Susan. Yes, he could still try to give her an extremely painful shock, but with so many people watching, it would be unlikely. He'd use better judgment simply because it would be in his own best interest. Sure, Tamara is much more fun to be around than Susan, but he'd have difficulty explaining to his boss why shifting responsibility for Tamara's project to Susan made any sense. But even if both Jeff and his boss were mania-cally biased, an impartial reviewer in HR, who would be responsible for administering the goal sheet process, would surely ask questions (and raise the issue a level if she felt it warranted further review).

As a final observation, we learned that Children in Need espoused such values as trust and integrity in its official policy literature, but the organization did not measure these attributes in their managers. If managers are not measured on attributes they are supposed to demon-strate, employees won't take these attributes seriously. In the case of Children in Need, the organization did not have any mechanism, such as an employee survey, to collect and assess feedback on how well the managers performed in areas like trust and integrity. Without it, a per-son like Jeff was free to be a poor manager out of simple neglect.

Are people in your company allowed to be poor managers?

PART II

The Blueprint for a Better Way

CHAPTER 5

Beyond the Group Hug
A Management Systems Approach

A new idea is often the result of two old ideas meeting for the first time. —ANONYMOUS

You might accept that the political workplace is highly destructive and might even have the battle scars to prove it. At the same time, you might feel skeptical about any attempt, even ours, to address it.

After your experiences in the workplace, you might be concerned that our approach is formulated on the well-worn premise that we should all just try to get along better or that we'll be espousing group hugs and the generous use of peppermint incense. Rest assured, that is not the case. Instead, our approach was inspired by some of the most hard-nosed management science developed over the past twenty years.

Although none of the concepts in this chapter were developed with the express purpose of eradicating the enemy within—far from it—they each make a contribution to achieving that goal. Simply combining and integrating these concepts would yield some valuable benefits, but they would not be enough to transform a political workplace. We must build on these foundations and construct an entirely new approach, one specifically designed to reform office politics. You won't see any of these specific concepts replayed later in this book, but you'll recognize their basic spirit in our approach.

Before reaching for the highly attractive but, some say, Pollyannaish goal of changing the political workplace, here's something to remember. You'll have to fight people's stubborn, glib notion that "you can't change that; it's just the way it is." In Rome, for example, corruption was so rampant that it never had a police force. The common belief was that the police would be bribed at every turn so their presence would serve no real purpose. That's just the way it was.

Later, in feudal Europe, if your father was a carpenter, you could never hope to be anything but a carpenter. If you were lucky enough to be born into the aristocracy, then your education, prestige, and wealth were simply handed over to you. That's just the way it was. The American dream of democracy was hundreds of years away, and even further off was women's suffrage, which leads us to a more modern example of another widely held immutable tenet.

Just a generation or two ago, people scoffed at the idea of women in the workplace holding down traditionally male jobs, like a firefighter or a doctor. Men went off to work, and women stayed home to raise children. That's just the way it was.

These illustrations all sound incredible, don't they? What were those people thinking? We've come such a long way that we forget that our way of living today was once regarded as an outrageous impossibility. At one point or another, you would have been considered naïve to believe a police force could be anything but absolutely corrupt, or that you could pursue any profession you desired, or that women could work outside the home.

Yet here we are. Collectively we shook off the stifling "That's just the way it is" sentiment and replied, "No, that's the way it is *only* if we allow it." And we are far better off for it. Let's make sure we carry on that lesson as we strive to replace the political workplace with one in which people who work hard and play by the rules win, people are rewarded based on merit, and people feel safe.

Warren Buffett's "Most Surprising Discovery"

Our approach is rooted in four well-established tenets, the first of which comes from a household name. Warren Buffett, the venerable stock picker and one of the richest men in the world, commented indirectly on the negative effects of office politics and the enemy within in one of his well-known and wisdom-filled annual reports.

While Mr. Buffett appears to be a serious, even brooding scholar most of the time, he likes to use his sardonic wit to drive home a point. In the case of his 1989 Berkshire Hathaway, Inc., *Annual Report,* he created a new business expression on the coattails of another.

The term *value imperative* conveys the simple idea that growing share-holder value—that is, keeping a company's stock price steadily rising along with the shareholder's personal wealth—is the imperative of any business. In essence, it is the invisible hand that guides all managers to make the best decisions for their companies all the time.

Recognizing the human frailties of poorly run companies, Warren Buffett twisted the term around and coined his own. The antithesis of the value imperative is what he termed the *institutional imperative,* or the political guiding force that causes otherwise smart people to make dumb decisions for their companies. In his report, he shares this bit of wit:

> *My most surprising discovery [in twenty-five years in business]: the overwhelming importance in business of an unseen force that we might call "the institutional imperative." In business school I was given no hint of the imperative's existence and I did not intuitively understand it when I entered the business world. I thought then that decent, intelligent, and experienced managers would automatically make rational business decisions. But I learned over time that isn't so. Instead, rationality frequently wilts when the institutional imperative comes into play.*[1]

Buffett understands that companies in the grasp of the institutional imperative make expensive mistakes based on little more than political whims. He points out, for example, "Any business craving of the leader, however foolish, will be quickly supported by detailed rate-of-return and strategic studies prepared by his troops."[2] Have you seen good money thrown after bad ideas to support some top dog's pet project? Apparently Mr. Buffett has, too.

He also asserts that these problems stem from what he calls "institutional dynamics" rather than "stupidity" on the part of individuals within those organizations. We'll cover those institutional dynamics at the end of this chapter and how they can be designed either to perpetuate a political environment and the enemy within or to build a safe, performance-driven workplace and drive shareholder value.

Fortunately for Warren Buffett and his investors, a few stand-out companies have structures and managers that minimize the institutional imperative's influence. Rather than accept the institutional imperative as simply being an inevitable part of any business, Buffett shrewdly chooses instead to concentrate his investments "in companies that appear alert to the problem."[3] That's Buffett's tongue-in-cheek way of saying that he avoids investing in companies that are overrun with office politics and the enemy within, or are governed by the "institutional imperative," as he would put it. Instead, he invests in companies whose strong institutional dynamics drive sound business decisions every day. These decisions build wealth rather than diminish it (which political decisions tend to do).

While it might seem somehow naïve to lament how commonplace office politics have become, you should recognize that highly successful companies work hard to overcome them. These companies are the ones in which Warren Buffett chooses to invest, and his strategy has paid off handsomely for him and for the stockholders of Berkshire Hathaway, Inc.

So what others call "office politics" or a "political environment," Warren Buffett calls "the institutional imperative." Regardless of the term used, they all describe the destructive force of the enemy within.

Value-Based Management

If what companies consciously need to work to avoid is the Warren Buffett–christened institutional imperative, what exactly should they be striving for?

Value-based management, the second well-established tenet in which our approach is grounded, provides an answer. The basic principle of value-based management, and arguably its most important contribution, is that a company's governing objective cannot be in doubt: *Its purpose is to build wealth for its owners* (that is, stockholders if it is a publicly traded company and individual owners if it is not). Companies as far afield as

Nordstrom, Boots, Dow Chemical, and Lloyd's Bank have embraced this ideal.

If the governing objective is to build wealth, then companies must eliminate those actions, decisions, policies, and principles that undermine this objective. Turf battles, one-upmanship, backbiting, masterminding, influence peddling, pet projects, personal egos, and all the other elements of a political workplace have no place in value-based management.

James McTaggart, Peter Kontes, and Michael Mankins's groundbreaking book, *The Value Imperative*, brought value-based management to the forefront. They assert that companies need to overcome both any *outside* competition and the "internal forces of the corporate institution" for a company to be successful and build wealth.[4] What's really needed, the authors say, is a formal management system to guide a company's decision making in its "battle against competition from the *outside* and the institutional imperative from the *inside.*"[5]

In fact, McTaggart, Kontes, and Mankins contend, without such a management system, any business is highly unlikely to be successful. That's how ubiquitous and powerful office politics are and how much at peril a company is for choosing to ignore the enemy within.

Open-Book Management

Open-book management is another well-established tenet in which our approach is grounded. Companies as varied as Sprint, Intel, the Body Shop, and the Chesapeake Corporation have embraced its philosophy. Open-book management recognizes that every employee on the payroll is in business all the time, whether *they* recognize it or not. The decisions they make, day in and day out, affect the company's financial performance. While no single decision might forever alter the company's fortunes, taken collectively, the daily decisions made across the enterprise drive the wealth creation (or wealth destruction) of the enterprise. While nobody disputes that this assertion is factually correct, few companies build their management systems around this simple truth. Open-book management does.

Open-book management subscribes to the notion that companies are in business to make money, and it is a way of running a business to get everyone in the company focused on making even more money. It is built on simple tenets: Get financial and operational information out to people and teach them how to use it, structure the company so people can act on what they know, and give people a stake in the company's success.

The objective is to get workers to think and act like businesspeople and owners instead of fiefdom builders and hired hands. One way to encourage this process is to make people partners in the enterprise and its success. Open-book managers understand the company's financials and share the risks if the company fails and the rewards if the company succeeds. Thus, this management style gets people involved and encourages them to assume responsibility rather than shirk from it. Once they understand how the company makes money, they'll know why certain kinds of behaviors are important.[6]

It's all fairly simple, but it's never easy. Most companies simply don't know how to effect this change, and they tend to stop short of changing their performance and incentive structures. It oftentimes takes a serious turn of fortune before a company is willing to do what's necessary and adapt. That was the case for the man who originally developed open-book management, a guy named Jack Stack. Here's his story.[7]

Stack and twelve other managers had bought out a division of International Harvester (now Navistar) known as the Renew Center, which remanufactured engines. The group was highly leveraged and couldn't afford to make a single mistake. Most executives in Stack's position would have gone to great lengths to keep the tenuous nature of their situation a secret from the troops. Most executives, then, would have been wrong.

Stack was convinced that the only way to survive was to tell all 119 employees about the company's shaky situation. So everyone in the organization could make the right decisions for the health of the company, he felt he had to let them know exactly where they stood, which was in an iffy place.

He began by distributing income statements, along with operational and budget numbers. He taught the managers and supervisors how to read them and what they meant. He helped them understand their jobs and how what they did every day impacted those numbers. For instance, he sat down with the operations managers and explained the link between increased productivity and the lower cost of goods sold. Managers, in turn, taught the people who worked for them and so on down the line.

Having everyone understand how the business worked and his or her individual role in it was a monumentally important step, but it wasn't enough. People had to have a stake in the success of the enterprise. So Stack developed a bonus plan and other incentive structures that were pegged to financial targets.

Stack thought that just like professional athletes, his employees needed certain things. They needed to understand the rules of the game, hence he gave them training in how the business worked. They needed to be able to follow the action, hence he distributed financial and operational reports. They needed to have a stake in winning, hence he offered the new incentive structure.

The result was success that extended well beyond Stack's fondest hopes. Sales grew by 40 percent a year, and the company's stock value rose from just $0.10 a share to $18.60 dollars in just ten years (a return of 18,500 percent for those of you who don't have a calculator nearby).

Stack's philosophy boiled down to a simple management system. First, make the numbers available, and teach people how to understand them. Then give them a chance to move the numbers they are able to affect. Offer them a share in the proceeds if the numbers move in the right direction, and the company will make more money. Rewarding people for making money teaches them that's what business is about. Finally, give them the right information and control of their job, and they can figure out how to make more profits.[8]

What does this system have to do with the *Insider's Rule Book* or office politics? Plenty. Navistar management created a powerful *Insider's Rule Book* to drive people to make smart decisions in the company's best interests. Rather than being loosely disjointed, as they typically are in a political environment, the individual's self-interest and the company's interests became tightly aligned.

Japanese Hoshin Planning

Our fourth and final basic tenet originated in the Far East. The term *hoshin* planning literally translated means "compass needle" and is meant to convey the process for setting the direction of a company. It was developed in the 1960s in Japan out of a growing sense of dissatisfaction with strategic planning. Today companies around the world, including Hewlett-Packard, Procter and Gamble, and Ford, embrace it.[9]

What bothered the Japanese managers wasn't the strategic plans themselves; it was the fact that they were so rarely actually executed (sound familiar?). While the best minds in business, and in the country at large, conceived of grand and glorious strategies, most of them wound up not worth the paper they were printed on, chiefly because they were never translated into actionable goals and objectives for individuals. They sat mutely on shelves and gathered dust.

Japanese managers quickly embraced Peter Drucker's historic *Management by Objectives,* but they found his theory didn't quite take them far enough. They needed a management system that could create and then cascade a high-level strategy down through the company, assigning progressively more specific goals at each level of management all the way down to the individual task level on the front lines. In this way, everyone in the organization could see how his or her individual goals fit into the company's overall goals and could understand his or her role in making the company successful.

Against this backdrop, hoshin planning was conceived. Its simple philosophy is to develop a shared vision for the company's future, to contrast it with the company's present, and then to build a detailed plan to close any gap between the two. Hoshin planning is unique because of its insistence that the process isn't complete until everyone in the organization understands his own goals, the tasks that he is personally accountable for, and how he fits into implementing the company's strategy.

For most companies, the planning process is confusing, ambiguous, and full of petty negotiations. Also, it means little to people in their daily work lives. In contrast, hoshin planning clearly details how every individual in the organization agrees to contribute, and it ensures a focus and convergence of all these individual efforts on the company's goals.[10]

These four basic tenets—the value imperative, value-based management, open-book management, and hoshin planning—all represent attempts to focus on doing the right thing for the business. In so doing, one can create an environment with the potential for transcending office politics. However, the eradication of the enemy within is only a possible by-product and not the specific aim of any of these management systems. That's why a new approach, building on these well-grounded concepts, is needed.

Fundamental Belief: It's All One System

Before previewing our strategy for creating shareholder value and a non-political workplace, we need to lay a little groundwork in regard to two fundamental beliefs. The first, which we call "One System," is described here.

Imagine for a moment that you've met an eccentric engineer who wants to start a car company. His idea is to begin with one of the world's best car engines, Ferrari. Then he wants to add one of the most respected transmissions around, Mercedes. Next, he adds an affordable body type, say, Ford, uses Volkswagen (VW) wheels; and installs a Lexus interior. He doesn't want to change a thing about these elements, not one single specification. He wants to buy them right off the factory floor and slap them together.

See any problems with that? I can think of one—the car won't work. A Ferrari engine simply isn't going to mesh with a Mercedes transmission, and a Ford body just won't fit. Common sense, right?

Well, many companies make a similar mistake. Creating a vision and strategy for a company—and actually executing it on a day-to-day basis—should all be part of one seamless system to run an organization and create shareholder value. But in reality, many companies fragment the processes, policies, and procedures that link strategy with execution. This lack of integration creates a leadership void that office politics quickly fill.

Here's how it typically happens. The company brings in a consulting firm to design a vision and strategy. Then the human resources department devises a bonus and compensation system. Next the finance department creates a planning or budgeting process to allocate resources. Somewhere along the line the company might form a project team to identify its key performance measures and design a performance management system.

To make matters worse, most companies don't follow the sequential process I described above (first developing a strategy, then turning to HR to craft a compensation program, and so on). For a company that's been around for a few years, these components have grown organically inside various departments and represent the status quo. From time to time, someone might win approval to redesign the planning process (the new transmission) or devise a new bonus program (the new body type), but nobody's crafted the entire system from beginning to end. The result? The car still won't run.

Companies wind up with a mishmash of loosely related processes, systems, and controls. While any one of these components might be the "best in its class," they simply won't work together in any way that's effective or reinforcing. In broad terms, people don't understand the strategy or the company's plan to achieve it, what role they play in it, or how they'll be rewarded for achieving it. The result is the company won't run properly, and office politics will again fill the void.

Let's take this analogy a step further. Imagine that the engineer has carefully redesigned everything in the new car with only one exception. We've got a Mercedes engine, a Mercedes transmission, a Mercedes body, and a Mercedes everything, almost. The only exception is that we still have VW wheels. Will the car work? No. It might sit in the driveway with the engine running, but it won't be able to move because VW wheels won't fit on a Mercedes axle.

So if we have a carefully coordinated strategy and operating plan—but the compensation program is disconnected—the company won't work effectively. Sure, it might idle in the driveway, but you won't be able to catch the competition zooming along the interstate.

The Rule of Law, Not Man

Another belief on which our strategy is founded is what's commonly referred to as "the rule of law." It speaks to an issue with which many companies struggle without even being fully aware of it.

The rule of man dominated all civilization up until recent times. Simply put, the rule of man dictates that the powerful can get away with what the weak cannot. In fact, the first written body of law—*Hammurabi's Code*—underscores this point. In ancient Babylon, for instance, the rape of an underclass woman by a rich man was not a crime, but if a rich man's wife was raped, it was a crime punishable by death. It almost didn't matter what the facts in a case were; if you were powerful enough, you could get away with anything.

In some countries, those run by dictators and despots, that's still the case. Those countries remain economically weak and isolated, but for the handful of people in charge, they're private playgrounds.

The United States was made great in part because it embraced the concept of the rule of law. Simply defined, the rule of law dictates that the same laws apply to everyone regardless of status or position (thus the statue representing justice is blindfolded). Rape is treated as rape, murder as murder, and theft as theft. It levels the playing field and makes living in a country governed by the rule of law safe and fair, especially when compared to a country dominated by the rule of man.

Incidentally, there is an economic implication here. An article published in the *Wall Street Journal* (2 January 1997) listed countries in which bribes are required for doing business. The article also pointed out that there is a clear correlation between a country's corruption factor and its economic development rating, with the most ethical countries worldwide enjoying the highest standards of living.

How would you characterize how your company operates? Politically driven companies operate under the rule of man. Here it's not what you know or what you're asking for, it's *who* you are that counts. The best-run companies we've studied and worked with, however, operate under the rule of law. These companies have standards, values, procedures, and policies that are applied fairly across the board. Determining what's in the organization's best interests drives their decisions, not who's for management and who's against them.

But once again, we need to address the *absence* of leadership. The rule of man is the unavoidable result for companies that lack *unambiguous* direction, accountability, goals, and rewards. We will deal with this issue in the balance of this book.

Notes

1 Warren Buffett, Berkshire Hathaway, Inc., *1989 Annual Report*, Omaha, Neb.

2 Ibid.

3 Ibid.

4 James McTaggart, Peter Kontes, and Michael Mankins, *The Value Imperative* (New York: The Free Press, 1994), 23.

5 Ibid., 42.

6 John Case, *Open-Book Management* (New York: HarperBusiness, 1996), 168.

7 Ibid., 32.

8 Ibid., 44.

9 Michael Cowley and Ellen Domb, *Beyond Strategic Vision* (Boston: Butterworth-Heinemann, 1997), 17.

10 Ibid., 29.

CHAPTER 6

Creating a New Sense of Purpose

Vision and Values

Destiny is not a matter of chance. It is a matter of choice. It is not a thing to be waited for, it is a thing to be achieved.
—WILLIAM JENNINGS BRYAN

Why are we here? What are we trying to achieve? The answers to those questions define a shared purpose and describe what "winning" means to an organization.

Silicon Valley is known for its start-ups and an almost messianic devotion to them. Sure, the lure of stock options that may spell instant retirement has something to do with it; but anyone who's been through it before will tell you, after six months or so, working eighteen hours a day, seven days a week gets old. For that level of dedication, you need greater motivation. For that level of dedication, you want to believe you're going to change the world, that somehow it's going to be a better place because you were here. That sense of being part of something larger than yourself is the *real* reason why you see superhuman effort in Silicon Valley and anywhere else start-ups flourish. It's also the reason why these companies can create so much shareholder value; it's often the result of a shared great vision rather than a stated aim in and of itself.

Great, you're thinking, *but since World War II, my company's been manufacturing tin containers for the consumer goods industry. What are we supposed to do?* That same sense of shared purpose, of being part of something larger than yourself, isn't restricted to leading-edge companies. It can be found in any organization in which workers embrace the company's vision and the values it espouses. That vision, and those values, doesn't have to be elaborate or complicated, either. I've seen companies highly motivate their workers with such simple ideas as treating all employees as owners, but these ideas only work when the companies actually follow through on them. Ultimately, a company's commitment to its goals and vision is what determines whether it successfully creates for its workers that motivating sense of belonging to something larger than themselves and the powerful dedication it engenders.

In this chapter we will describe a step-by-step process to create a vision for an organization and a set of values to support it. We'll also specify how to involve the organization in the process to improve its communication and commitment. But even more important, we'll begin to describe a highly effective methodology to actualize these shared visions and values.

Along the way we'll also have fun. Trust me.

How to Create a Shared Vision

Okay, you run a six-person Internet company or a sixty-thousand–person steel company. You want to create a vision for the organization, one that will inspire and lead your people to improve their performance. Where do you start?

The Collage Warm-Up Exercise

You'll need to figure out *who* you want to participate in drafting the vision and *how* they're going to do it. The *how* question we will answer in detail, but we can only give you guidelines about the *who* question.

You will want no more than six to eight people to start with. Going past that number can get unwieldy. Now who gets invited is your choice, but I urge you to use a mix of senior and junior people from different parts of the organization. This selection will matter later on when you share the vision with the rest of the enterprise and people ask, "Who put this together?" You don't want people to think it was just the most senior people or just the marketing people or just the engineers. Otherwise, it becomes *their* vision. Having a broad mix of people develop the vision is the first step in making it a *shared* vision.

Of course, you want to choose people who are bright, well respected, and able to think beyond their role in the business. I could go on, but you probably already have a sense for who should be there.

Schedule a morning for this exercise and invite them. *Only a morning?* you wonder. Yes, if it's well structured and facilitated, that's all the time you'll need. When you share your vision with the rest of the organization, you'll need much more time.

For this exercise, you'll need a couple dozen magazines of different types and for each attendee one big sheet of white construction paper, scissors, and glue.

The idea is quite simple. Give everyone thirty minutes to look through the magazines for images or words that represent what they would like to see as the organization's future, say five years out. Remind them that they'll need to reserve some time to cut out the words or pictures they want and glue them on the construction paper.

Thirty minutes might not seem like much time, and it's not. That's intentional. You don't want people to overthink this part; you're going for a visceral reaction, which the time pressure enhances. If you gave them four hours, some people's collage would wind up looking like a ransom note with letters and words cut out to form paragraphs of exacting precision. That's decidedly *not* what you want.

The next step is to put everybody's artwork up on a wall. Have one person volunteer to go first. Have each participant then describe what he or she sees in the collage and how he or she interprets it. Then have the person who created the collage tell everyone what she was actually trying to convey. When this is done, go on to the next person and continue until everyone's collage has been discussed.

The level of discussion will go far beyond what you're used to seeing. Rather than standard talk of growth rates and market share, people will reveal the type of workplace they want to be part of, the higher good the organization can contribute to the community and the world at large, and simply how good they will feel to work there.

The Newspaper Article Exercise

That first exercise, the collage experience, is meant as an "appetizer" of sorts. The intent is to whet people's appetite for thinking creatively and to allow them to "get crazy."

Think of the second exercise, then, as the main meal. It's designed to build on the excitement generated by the first exercise and to help the group "get real."

To begin the exercise, have the same group of people answer the following question: It's five years from now, and *Time* magazine is doing a story on our company/organization, highlighting our success. What does the author say?

Choose a "scribe" to record everyone's ideas. Then let each person take a turn and provide one comment. Ask everyone to phrase their statements in the present tense. For example, "people love to work there, and XYZ Company has the lowest turnover in the industry."

As each person speaks, the scribe writes down his or her comment on an oversize Post-it with a bold felt-tip marker and places it on the wall. After everyone has contributed, ask them to do another round and give more answers. Usually somewhere between four and eight rounds, when people feel like they're repeating themselves, it's time to end the exercise.

Finding the Elements

The next step is to organize these individual Post-its by themes. Have one person group the Post-it comments by physically moving them, and ask her to explain the theme that she sees. Have her write the theme on another Post-it as a title card and place it above her grouping.

Ask the next person if he wants to change anything in the grouping. If he does, he must explain why and move the cards. He might move a card between existing groups or create a new group. To keep it simple, if people disagree about the placement of a card, copy it so that it can appear under more than one group. It's really the themes you're trying to identify here.

Then let the next person group the cards. By the fourth or fifth person's turn, there's been so much discussion about the themes that very few changes are made to the groupings.

After everyone has taken a turn, the group reviews the final result. When it's done, it might look something like figure 6-1.

Writing the Statement

Now that you've established the individual themes describing the future everyone wants to see for the organization, the next step is to craft your vision statement. While some groups write their vision statements as prose in paragraph form, others use just bullet points. I've even seen one that combined images from the collage exercise combined with text to describe the vision. No matter what you choose, the spirit and intent of the vision themes developed in the newspaper exercise needs to be reflected in the final vision statement.

It's not an exact science; draft your best shot, or give it to the person in the group who aspires to be a writer. The important thing is to capture the original sprit of the vision and its key elements. Once it's done, get out there and share it with the rest of the organization.

Sharing It with the World

Some people use the term *validating the vision* to describe this part of the experience, but I like to think of it more as *sharing* the vision. If you had tried to validate one of history's best-known visions—the Kennedy administration's dream to develop the means within one decade to put a man on the moon and return him safely to earth—NASA engineers would have told you it was unrealistic and maybe even impossible. Great visions inspire people because they encourage them to go beyond what they think they're capable of. A simple dream—for example, to go to the grocery store and return with a quart of milk—is realistic enough but not very inspirational.

FIGURE 6-1
Finding the Elements

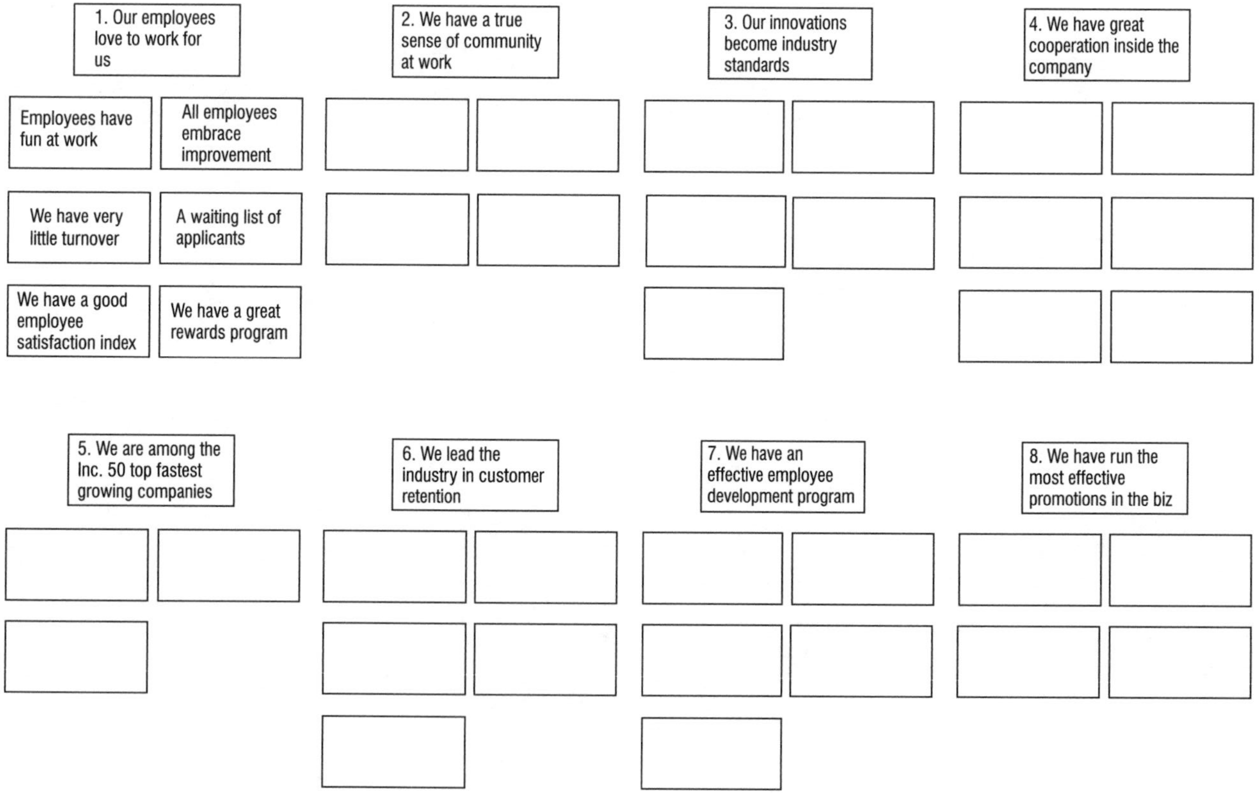

1. Our employees love to work for us

Employees have fun at work

All employees embrace improvement

We have very little turnover

A waiting list of applicants

We have a good employee satisfaction index

We have a great rewards program

2. We have a true sense of community at work

3. Our innovations become industry standards

4. We have great cooperation inside the company

5. We are among the Inc. 50 top fastest growing companies

6. We lead the industry in customer retention

7. We have an effective employee development program

8. We have run the most effective promotions in the biz

A candle hidden under a basket does no good, nor does a vision kept secret in the boardroom. People have to know what the company's vision is in order to be inspired by it, right? Now you have to determine the best way to introduce it.

First of all, face-to-face contact beats any other means for sharing a vision. Don't start by sending out e-mail messages, writing columns for the company newsletter, or handing out the vision on laminated cards. Instead, schedule a series of town hall–style meetings to reach as many people as you reasonably can. Tell them about how you developed the vision, what you discussed, and what the group finally proposed. Then solicit responses. If you conducted the process in a sincere, open way, you shouldn't have any problems.

The point here is to start a dialogue about the vision. Does it touch people's hearts and deep desires? How? What does it mean to them? How would they explain it to their families? What would it feel like if they could make even half of it come true?

You want people to understand what the vision is all about, but you want them to commit to it as well. After all, this shared vision will be what keeps them going when they're at the office late at night to make a deadline or when they're listening to an irate customer.

It will also be an important part of what enables them to work with their colleagues as partners rather than as political opponents. Simply put, sharing the same broad vision helps them transcend narrow differences. Of course, it's not the only thing necessary to accomplish that goal.

••

How to Create Shared Values

Defining a set of shared values means determining what workers in an organization care about. Combining it with the organization's vision will provide a clear sense of purpose for the members of the organization (especially if the values and vision are converted into concrete action, as we will discuss in chapters 7 and 8).

Simple Questions, Valuable Answers

The process for defining a set of shared values is similar to that for creating a compelling vision for the organization. First, determine who should participate. Some companies choose to use the same group of people that created the vision, while others bring in a separate group. Either way is acceptable, but I prefer using the same group because these people are more intimately aware of the vision, which can serve as their guide.

Once you have the group together, schedule a morning and run through a simple exercise. Review the vision with everyone, and ask the members to answer the following question: As an organization, what will we need to value to be competitive *and* achieve our vision?

The question has two parts because both ideas are essential to the organization's ultimate success. Your group members need to recognize that they are not alone in this world (market) and that competitors, the real enemy, will always be willing to take their customers and their profits. Our vision, then, won't mean much if we're not around to make it happen. So they need to figure out what they need to value to be competitive and fight another day to achieve their greater vision.

Once they've crafted a solid vision and people are fired up to achieve it, they'll have a head start on the competition. Likewise, if they are sufficiently competitive, then they can achieve the financial success necessary to fund a greater vision. To go a step further, the vision itself might include attaining financial success (I often think that it should), and determining what's needed to be competitive in that case is directly tied to achieving the vision.

Once you've posed the question above, go around the room and ask every person to make a single contribution. Again, have the group's scribe write each comment down on an oversize Post-it and put it on the wall. Go around the room and ask for contributions until the group feels all the major points have been captured.

At this point, you might have twenty, thirty, or even more value statements on the wall. This number is way too many to be of any practical use. You'll want to narrow the list down to about ten priority values, or those ideas that will drive the business and its leaders. A few exercises, the first of which you already know, will help get you to that point.

Finding the Themes

Similar to what your group did in creating the vision, you'll need to group like statements into themes. Again, have one person group the Post-it comments by physically moving them, and let her explain the theme that she sees. Ask her to write the theme as a title card and to place it above the grouping.

Then ask the next person if he wants to change anything, which he can do by moving a card between existing groups or creating a new group. Continue until everyone has taken a turn, and then let the group review the final result.

At this point, there might still be an unmanageable number of value statements. Any more than fifteen is difficult for people to remember and therefore not effective. Next you'll need to prioritize them. You can do this task by using a couple of handy tools.

Prioritizing Them

The first exercise you can utilize is called a driver diagram. Simply put, place all of the header cards (those that group statements into themes) on a flip chart. Then point to any one of the values and ask the group, "Does this first value actually drive any other values?" You want to identify *major* influences here, not subtleties. If the answer is yes, draw an arrow between the values to indicate that relationship. Then ask if any of the other values drive this first value. Once again, draw an arrow indicating any relationships.

You have completed the exercise when you have evaluated each value this way and you have a diagram illustrating the drivers. The values with the most arrows emanating from them have the high potential values. The final result might look something like figure 6-2. In this simplified example, value *E* is a major driver of the other values. It is a clear priority.

Another tool that you can use to help prioritize the identified values is called a gap analysis. First, draw a large circle on a flip chart. Then place the values around the circle's perimeter. Put a dot in the center of the circle, and draw a line connecting the dot to each of the values along the perimeter.

For each value, ask the group, "Are we currently demonstrating this value as best as we possibly can?" If the group answers with a resounding yes, put an *X* on the perimeter. If the opposite is true, put an *X* in the center. When the answer lies somewhere in between, mark it appropriately on the continuum. Now connect all of the *X*s with a line. The gap between

FIGURE 6-2
Sample Driver Diagram

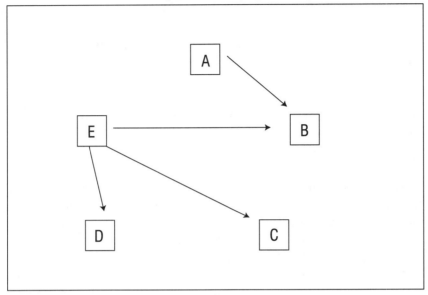

the circle's perimeter and the lines you've just drawn represents the disparity between the ideal and what currently exists, and the largest gaps show perhaps the greatest opportunities for improvement. Figure 6-3 is an example of the finished product. In this simplified example, C is the value with the greatest gap between current reality and desired reality.

Using either one of these tools, or a combination, the group needs to determine the top ten priority values the company must demonstrate on an ongoing basis to be successful in terms of both being competitive and realizing its vision. You don't have to limit them to ten values; however, the group must determine its priorities, which, frankly, is impossible once they near twenty "top" values. So use your judgment on the exact number of priority values you want to reach. Just make certain they are all clearly differentiated, highly desirable, and easy to understand.

At the end of this exercise, you will have identified a list of priority values that everyone in the enterprise, especially its leaders, will need to demonstrate on a consistent basis. Figure 6-4 is an example of priority values a client in the financial services industry uses.

FIGURE 6-3
Sample of a Gap Analysis

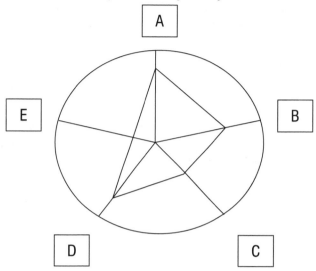

FIGURE 6-4
Sample List of Priority Values

To be successful in realizing our vision and remaining competitive, NuCo Company must embrace and have the highest standards for:

❑ Modeling Trust and Integrity
❑ Pursuing Constructive Collaboration
❑ Treating People with Respect
❑ Upholding Diversity
❑ Creating Innovative Solutions
❑ Driving Results
❑ Acting Strategically
❑ Meeting and Exceeding Customer Expectations
❑ Demonstrating Honesty, Truthfulness, and Openness
❑ Analytical and Conceptual Thinking
❑ Taking Decisive Action
❑ Managing Change

While some of these values are self-descriptive, others are less so. People need to understand them in the context of the company's vision and its assessment of what the company needs to do to stay competitive.

Getting the Word Out

As with the vision statement, you will need to communicate the organization's values to everyone. Again town hall–style meetings are an excellent venue for personal interaction and a sense of give-and-take. Come prepared to discuss how you identified the values and your rationale for selecting them out of all the other possibilities.

Another highly effective way to get the word out is to "train the trainers." This process means hand selecting a small group of people to immerse themselves in the intricacies of how and why the values were identified. These people can then teach other small groups, who, in turn, teach others still. In a relatively brief period, everyone in the organization can participate in a small-group experience.

You can implement this train-the-trainer concept numerous different ways. You can include each functional head in the first training group, and the process can then cascade down along functional lines. Alternatively, you can follow a business or geography or any number of other lines. You can decide what's best for your enterprise based on how your company is organized and on other cultural considerations.

Customers, Vendor Partners, Suppliers

Although having a shared vision and values can produce a potent competitive advantage, if only for its organizing and focusing worth, the company needs to exercise them openly. Acting consistently with the shared vision and values is imperative to their overall effectiveness. If people see that these values and vision can be disregarded without consequence, that they only need to pay them lip service, then their existence will cause the company more harm than good. People's cynicism and disillusionment will skyrocket.

To put it bluntly, companies need to be kept honest. It's easy for managers to say they value honesty and openness, but then clam up when it comes to anticipated layoffs. We'll cover this issue more thoroughly in chapters 8 and 9, but we can take a first step here.

First, share your company's vision and values with your *customers.* They might catch some of the excitement a great vision can induce and feel more committed to your organization. I've seen this reaction a number of times. Even a customer can feel a part of something larger than himself just by being associated with your company. One reason why Apple Computer originally caused huge excitement (and still does to some extent) was that its customers shared in the feeling of being part of a David versus Goliath story as Apple competed with IBM. Apple was poised to put a computer in every home, and ordinary people wanted to share in the revolution.

Next, share your vision and values with your *suppliers.* Your contacts there are people just like yourself, although in sterile business communications that fact can be lost. Apart from seeing your organization as a means to pay their bills, your suppliers also have a desire to be part of something special, which your company might represent. Even more important, if they work closely enough with you, they can tell you if you're going astray. You need to tell them, "If we're acting inconsistently with our vision and values, let us know."

Finally, this same rationale supports sharing your vision and values with your *vendor partners,* or those organizations with which you share business. They'll be sure to tell you if you're acting inconsistently because it might ultimately impact their own business. But in addition to keeping you honest, your vendor partners will also share in the excitement of being connected to a higher purpose. They might even offer some insight to help make the vision a reality.

So share your new vision and values with people outside the company, or "stakeholders," as they are often called. They can help build on your excitement and sense of purpose and ensure congruence between your words and actions.

While this information sharing can be an excellent first step in ensuring consistency between value statements and actual behavior, you also need a well-defined mechanism to secure it. That's the subject of chapter 7.

CHAPTER 7

Developing New Leaders
You Get What You Measure

Conviction is worthless unless it is converted into conduct.
—THOMAS CARLYLE

The key question this chapter addresses is how to convert conviction, as captured in the organization's stated vision and values, into concrete conduct. In many respects, your company's success hinges on this key issue.

Imagine for a moment working for an organization and listening to senior management describe a new set of values it wants all workers to embrace. It sounds great to hear management say, "We're going to open up communications and treat people with respect and dignity."

But after a few weeks you notice that your coworkers haven't really changed their behavior. People still get ambushed in meetings, sales forecasts are just as unrealistic, department heads won't share their resources, and everyone guards their information just as jealously as before. You observe the stated values' incongruence with actual values, and you notice no one suffers any consequences. For all of management's talk about change, nobody is held accountable for it.

Now how do you feel? Perhaps you feel the way you did when you discovered there is no Santa Claus. This analogy is even more appropriate than it is funny. If you've recently joined the work world and this is your first experience with a company espousing one thing but doing another, you're going to be quite disappointed. Moreover, experienced coworkers are going to tell you that you were naïve even to think it could turn out any other way. "Of course they didn't mean it," they'll say. "Why did you believe them in the first place?"

You'll emerge from this experience a little bit older and a little bit wiser. You'll also be more callous, cynical, and disbelieving of your management. If your company ever tries to inject new values again, you'll join the many others who scoff and roll their eyes.

This scenario is played out all too frequently; it's one of the most common mistakes that organizations make. Nothing will harm company morale more than workers finding their managers act by one set of values while they espouse another. In this chapter, we'll describe how to avoid that crucial mistake and ensure congruence between rhetoric and reality.

How to Develop New Leaders

To develop new leaders, you first need to define the behaviors and characteristics you want your people to exhibit. The tool for assessing your people that you will create here is a leadership appraisal form.

Creating Headlines

What characteristics does your organization want in its people, especially its leaders? What types of behavior should they exhibit? The answers lies in the work you did in the previous chapter.

First, you need to define who will participate in this selection process. Too often this type of assignment is handed off to a human resources executive, which is a big mistake. You want people who live and breathe the business every day, and HR professionals can be a little removed from ordinary workday concerns. Moreover, you need broader representation.

You want a cross-functional team at a fairly senior level to undertake this task. Frankly, this group can spot the type of ivory-tower nonsense that can insert itself into this process and steer clear of it. Furthermore, the final "product" this type of cross-functional team proposes will be both effective and respected. In my experience, everyone can spot the difference in results from an HR-only team and from a cross-functional one.

Your team's first task is to review the organization's values and vision statements. Then they'll need to come up with a quick "headline" description for each value. Figure 7-1 is an example that uses the same values identified in figure 6-4. Although chapter 6 listed more values, I think you get the point with these few examples. You need brief, honest, and concise descriptions. They need to convey immediately the essence of the stated values.

Assessing Proficiency

You've done the easy (or at least easier) part, and it's tempting to think, you're done. But if you stop here, people won't know enough about what is expected of them to change their behavior much beyond paying lip service to these newly christened values. In addition, your ultimate aim is to evaluate individuals' performance based on these criteria, so you'd better ensure these characteristics are defined well enough to be assessed.

We recommend creating three broad levels of performance within each characteristic. They can be as simple as "exceeds expectations," "meets expectations," and "does not meet expectations." Corresponding to each of these three levels are statements that convey what the person being evaluated must do to demonstrate that level of performance. If

FIGURE 7-1
NuCo Company Value Headlines

Constructive Collaboration Means   Working with others to develop plans, opinions, and decisions that will affect them or the organization.

Decisive Action Means   Making sound decisions under time pressure, or conditions of uncertainty, where all the data isn't available.

Driving Results Means   Driving the actual execution of strategies and plans to achieve organizational objectives.

Trust and Integrity Means   Modeling our company's values consistently and at all times.

Treating People with Respect Means   Demonstrating sensitivity in dealing with others, seeking to understand other people's feelings, and acting on their concerns.

someone exceeds expectations in the category of constructive collaboration, what exactly is he doing? What sets him apart from someone who just meets expectations?

Determining these levels is obviously hard work, and you might want some outside help on this part, but never hand over control or responsibility for this stage of the effort. Although an outside consultant might facilitate the work, it ultimately needs to come from your own people; they need to feel the ownership.

Figure 7-2 is an example that measures the behaviors people demonstrate in the constructive collaboration category. You'll notice we used five levels—L1 through L5—rather than three. Because in the real world your people will tend to fall somewhere between the lines rather than fall solidly in any one performance category, our solution is to have five levels that span the three performance categories. That way you can recognize when someone comes in at the high (L1) or the low (L2) end of, say, the exceeds expectations measure.

FIGURE 7-2
Assessing Constructive Collaboration Behaviors

Constructive Collaboration—Working with others to develop plans, opinions, and decisions that will affect them or the organization.

EXCEEDS EXPECTATIONS		MEETS EXPECTATIONS	DOES NOT MEET EXPECTATIONS	
L1	L2	L3	L4	L5
• Consistently develops and maintains cooperative working relationships		• Persuasively presents ideas	• Hesitates to share information and resources	
• Looks for "win-win" solutions		• Willingly shares information with others	• Delays or causes delays	
• Persuades others by uncovering shared benefits		• Helps others as asked, occasionally even without being asked	• Seldom considers how others will react to his/her ideas	
• Strives to achieve broad "buy in" from others rather than simply a go-ahead by a senior person		• Proactively involves others in decisions that might impact them	• Fails to present ideas in a manner compelling to others	

Let's look at another example. Figure 7-3 shows how a company might evaluate trust and integrity.

The idea here is to think through the types of behavior that model each one of your company's values. Then you'll need to grade these behaviors in a way that clearly identifies exemplary behavior from mediocre or even unacceptable behavior.

The 360-Degree Evaluation

Okay, you've outlined your company's values and developed a way to assess the performance of any individual in the company against those values. But who's to say whether *you* are currently performing at an L2 level or an L4 level on the trust and integrity competency? If it's just your boss, aren't you back in the same position as before, needing to respond to your boss's changing whims and the politics that engenders?

FIGURE 7-3
Assessing Trust and Integrity Behaviors

Trust and Integrity—Modeling company values consistently and at all times.

EXCEEDS EXPECTATIONS		MEETS EXPECTATIONS	DOES NOT MEET EXPECTATIONS	
L1	L2	L3	L4	L5
• Identifies lack of congruence between personal and organizational values and speaks out		• Is open and candid with others	• Conveys situations in a manner that conceals or obfuscates problems	
• Is perceived as a highly trusted person		• Behaves consistently with the organization's shared values	• Exhibits inconsistency between words and actions	
• Confronts others whose behavior is inconsistent with the organization's shared values		• Is ethical and honest in all business dealings	• Gives credit to others, but not uniformly	
• Speaks up for what is right		• Freely gives credit to others and accepts responsibility for mistakes	• Does the right thing only if watched	

The answer is to use a 360-degree evaluation, completed by a sampling of subordinates, peers, and, yes, superiors. Depending on your position, of course, perhaps two peers along with an equal number of subordinates, your boss, and perhaps another superior or two will evaluate your performance. Somewhere between six and eight evaluations will provide a more well-rounded view of your performance against the organization's shared values than any single (perhaps biased) perspective.

I'll describe how it works here, but this instance is where some outside help can really be useful. Having participated in 360-degree evaluations before, I can tell you that sending off an evaluation you filled out for a peer to an out-of-town (or at least out-of-the-building) address ensures anonymity, a key requirement for an effective program.

To conduct a 360-degree evaluation, you simply need to send worksheets, such as figures 7-4 and 7-5, to the individual being evaluated (so she can complete one for herself) and those people evaluating her. Figure

FIGURE 7-4
Instructions for NuCo Company Leadership Appraisal Form

You are being asked to evaluate the leadership competencies of [insert name], as defined in the NuCo Company Values Statement.

KEY
L1 = Exceeds Expectations
L2 = Meets Expectations (+)
L3 = Meets Expectations
L4 = Meets Expectations (−)
L5 = Does Not Meet Expectations

For each leadership competency listed, please review the examples of behavior that appear for L3: Meets Expectations (see attachment for descriptions). If the person being reviewed exhibits many of the behaviors listed under the "Meets Expectations" category, or similar ones, then he or she is performing at the L3: Meets Expectations level. If the person being evaluated demonstrates more effective behaviors than those listed under L3, but not quite those listed under L1: Exceeds Expectations, then he or she is performing at the L2: Meets Expectations (+) level. If he or she exhibits behaviors less effective than those listed under L3: Meets Expectations, but not as ineffective as those listed under L5: Does Not Meet Expectations, then he or she is operating at an L4: Meets Expectations (−) level. The behaviors are only examples; the employee does not have to demonstrate each one associated with a category in order to achieve that rating.

FIGURE 7-5
NuCo Company Leadership Appraisal Form

Date: _____

Name of Person Being Evaluated: _____

Name of Person Evaluating (held confidential): _____
Department: _____

KEY
L1 = Exceeds Expectations
L2 = Meets Expectations (+)
L3 = Meets Expectations
L4 = Meets Expectations (−)
L5 = Does Not Meet Expectations

BEHAVIORS	RATING
Trust and Integrity	_____
Constructive Collaboration	_____
Treating People with Respect	_____
Diversity	_____
Creating Innovative Solutions	_____
Driving Results	_____
Acting Strategically	_____
Meeting or Exceeding Customer Expectations	_____
Honesty, Truthfulness, Openness	_____
Analytical and Conceptual Thinking	_____
Decisive Action	_____
Managing Change	_____

7-4 is a sample set of instructions, and figure 7-5 is a sample appraisal form.

Now comes the fun part. After all the results are in, you'll be able to compare how you judge yourself versus how others see you. The gaps in perception indicate areas that need your serious consideration, especially those areas that were rated uniformly low.

There are many different ways to illustrate these gaps. See figure 7-6 for one example. In this case, the person being evaluated has a higher opinion of himself than his colleagues do. He thinks he rates highly in the trust and integrity category, but his colleagues beg to differ, just as they do on the constructive collaboration category. On the treating people with respect dimension, everybody agrees that he's just meeting expectations.

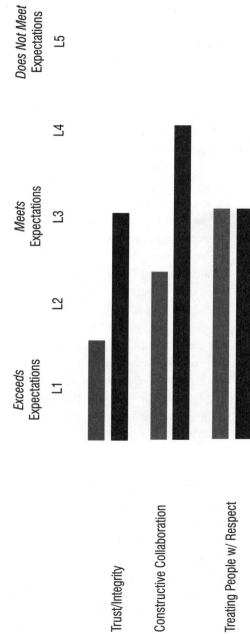

FIGURE 7-6
Sample 360-Degree Evaluation Gap Analysis

NuCo Financial
360-Degree Evaluation
Ratings Gap Analysis
Prepared for [Insert Name]

Thus far, we have translated values into specific behaviors and found a way to assess individuals' performance on these dimensions. But one question remains: Why should your workers care what their performance assessments say?

Links to Rewards

Chapter 9 covers rewards, but it's worth pausing here to emphasize one specific aspect—how they tie into the organization's values.

Until this point, anyone who feigned interest in the organization's values but did not really adhere to them could do so without much personal cost. Sure, he might be subjected to a little browbeating from superiors and embarrassed over scoring poorly on an issue like trust and integrity, but like most of us, he could deal with that. A handful of people (we've all met at least one) would even actually be proud of scoring poorly on a dimension like treating people with respect, because it would reinforce their reputations of being real SOBs. These same people, unintentionally perhaps, make a mockery of the organization's objectives and slowly turn everyone else into cynics of the process. Without some form of material consequence, then "values" and "leadership behaviors" become meaningless buzzwords.

Your organization has many ways to link behaviors with rewards. The simplest way is to make the 360-degree evaluation part of the annual performance review and tie some part of the merit increase formula to the evaluation's scores. Perhaps the score could drive one-quarter or even one-half of a person's merit increase on her leadership appraisal.

Another easy way to link the leadership appraisal to rewards is to make attaining certain scores on particular parts of the evaluation a requirement for being eligible for promotion. As an example, anyone aspiring to manage a group of more than three people must have at least an L3 rating on the honesty, truthfulness, and openness competency and an L2 rating on trust and integrity. Anyone aspiring to be a senior director, let's say, needs a minimum rating of L2 on driving results. You can change these requirements, of course, to accommodate different circumstances, but your modifications should be well reasoned and well communicated.

One indirect way of linking rewards to the leadership appraisal is to incorporate it into the personal development process. As part of the management process, many companies ask their managers to identify the development needs of their direct reports once a year. The managers can highlight large gaps in the 360-degree evaluations as development needs and then identify personal development plans to address them.

Of course, if your company has a bonus system, that might be the most direct way to influence behavior. The results of the leadership appraisal can drive certain portions of the bonus calculation. In some companies, half of the bonus rests on this type of evaluation; for other companies, it's closer to 10 percent.

The point here is simply that some people, perhaps most of us, need a material reward linked to leadership behaviors in order to take them seriously. While there are some altruistic individuals who, by their very nature, always want to do the right thing for the organization, the rest of us need a bit more encouragement.

Celebrating Model Leaders

Apart from material rewards, workers of every level respond to examples. Look at your organization. Who exactly is being celebrated and for what?

A few years ago a large and well-known consulting firm launched a program called Work/Life Balance. It was initiated as a result of a year-long effort to understand why the firm's retention rate was so low, especially among highly desirable consultants. The study concluded that consultants left the firm mainly because of a lack of balance between their work and home lives. The time spent away from home, either at work or traveling, was just way too much for many people.

So the firm formed the Work/Life Balance program ostensibly to address this issue. Without going into detail, it launched numerous "voluntary" programs, which consultants could theoretically opt into. The problem was nobody seemed to take advantage of these programs, and the retention rate continued to slide.

What went wrong? The firm publicly celebrated those consultants who demonstrated the more traditional role instead of those who enrolled in the voluntary programs. As an example, at a semiannual "all hands" meeting, the managing director praised a woman who had billed 100 hours a week for six consecutive months. Neither the quality of her work nor her contribution to the company she was on assignment with was ever mentioned. He only celebrated the sheer number of hours she was willing to work.

In another example, the firm's quarterly magazine ran a cover story on a consultant who slept just four hours a night, was traveling to three separate cities each week for three separate assignments, and was able to write and publish a business book "in his spare time."

What were the messages here? The rank-and file consultants in that particular firm easily concluded that the voluntary programs were not for those employees who were serious about their careers and wanted to continue to demonstrate their commitment to the firm.

One of the world's largest financial services firms had a decidedly different approach to celebrating leaders. The company went through the same process as in our NuCo Company example—identifying desired leadership traits, defining specific measures for them, assessing employees' capabilities, and so on. Then, each year people were free to choose from among their peers someone who had demonstrated the best of any one leadership trait and to submit that person's name and story to an awards nominating committee. That group selected 100 finalists. At the end of the year, the finalists from all over the world congregated for a special two-day celebration.

In 2000, the event was held in New York City, with Bill Cosby as the keynote speaker. A dinner dance the first night was followed by an awards ceremony the next day. To make the event even more memorable, the award winners were asked to gather on stage, where they could be filmed by television cameras. The live feed aired on the Sony Jumbotron television in Times Square for tens of thousands of people to see. With this type of congruence between stated values and celebrated values, it is no surprise that this company finds its employees "living the values" every day.

The Role of Training

You have defined the leadership traits you want your managers to exhibit every day, devised measurements of these traits, and developed a means to evaluate your managers' performance against these measures. You have given a reason for people to care, beyond a sense of altruism, about the company's values and vision by linking performance with rewards and by celebrating model leaders. Are you done? Not quite.

While I've never subscribed to the notion that there are "natural born leaders," I do think some people have an innate connection with certain desired leadership behaviors, and they act on their convictions accordingly. In that sense, *they* are "natural leaders"—good for them—but everyone else needs a little help to develop their leadership abilities.

Let's look at one more example of desired leadership behaviors at NuCo Company. Figure 7-7 examines behaviors that drive results. Looking through this evaluation, you can see how someone who lacks project management skills would not fare well. Although determination counts for a great deal, it's no substitute for basic project management skills. For

FIGURE 7-7
Assessing Driving Results Behaviors

Driving Results—Driving the actual execution of strategies and plans to achieve organizational objectives.

EXCEEDS EXPECTATIONS		MEETS EXPECTATIONS	DOES NOT MEET EXPECTATIONS	
L1	L2	L3	L4	L5
• Is persistent in working to meet objectives in the face of challenges and obstacles		• Develops project plans	• Does not establish priorities or stick to them once they are established	
• Always completes projects on time		• Conveys a sense of urgency to others	• Spends more effort explaining delays and other obstacles than on working to overcome them	
• Establishes key milestones to ensure progress		• Accurately estimates resources required to support projects	• Meets some deadlines, but is not consistent	
• Consistently demonstrates commitment to meet objectives		• Commits to deadlines and works to meet them	• Underestimates resources required to meet project objectives	

example, knowing how to build a project plan is essential to running almost any project.

Encourage those who have not scored well in this metric to attend a course on project planning. They'll learn all about setting key milestones, prioritizing activities and tasks to complete a project, and estimating the required resource needs.

If you switch gears and review the constructive collaboration metric, you could offer training opportunities in such areas as building effective presentation skills, polishing interpersonal skills, and so on. Some of this same training, plus other skills, could be beneficial in addressing the trust and integrity values.

The point here is not to leave people hanging, unable to move ahead, but to give them the support that they need to be successful. After all, what distinguishes the "old world" most from this one is fairness, and nothing is more fair than helping those who want to help themselves.

Now that you have developed new leaders, you have to give them something valuable to do. Setting and achieving goals are the subjects of the next chapter.

CHAPTER 8

Drawing a New Road Map
Nonpolitical Goal Setting and Planning

If you don't plan where you're going, you'll probably wind up somewhere else. —ANONYMOUS

Thus far, we've established that the enemy within flourishes when the following three simple questions go unanswered: What needs to be accomplished? What are the workers' individual roles in achieving that And what's in it for them? To reform the enemy within, we've determined, we must rewrite the *Insider's Rule Book* and answer these questions directly.

Before you can address the *Insider's Rule Book* for your company, we need to review how companies set their goals and make plans for achieving them. All too often we see a disconnect between what the company needs to accomplish and what their workers' roles are in that effort. Instead, there is a confusing mix of (sometimes competing) goals, objectives, and targets. One of the first things I like to do when working with a company is ask people what they're working on and in what direction they are headed. If I had to diagram what I usually see, it would look something like figure 8-1.

The problem I see isn't that they're doing something wrong; it's just

FIGURE 8-1
Work Focus Diagram of a Typical Organization

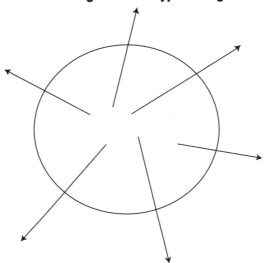

that people are headed in different directions. Here the workers are un-likely to make significant progress in any one particular direction, and they have no sense of being a part of their company's collective purpose.

What the company needs, instead, is a process that staples together a broad vision, and its corresponding individual goals, with simple mecha-nisms to make it happen. Then the company can align all of its workers' efforts, or arrows, as seen in figure 8-2.

For your organization to meet this overall objective, you'll first need to determine how to establish the company's goals. Then you'll need to examine how to develop the plans to meet these targets. Last, you'll lay out a process for allocating resources to ensure these plans are properly funded.

What do all of these decisions have to do with office politics? Every-thing. The enemy within will fill the leadership void created when these three fundamental processes are poorly run or inadequately integrated (or when the arrows are misaligned). It would be nice if your organization's CEO could just send out a memo urging everyone to get along for the common good, but we know it wouldn't work.

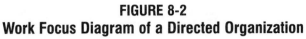

FIGURE 8-2
Work Focus Diagram of a Directed Organization

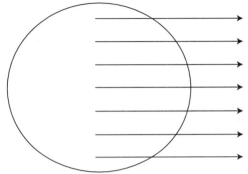

Thus, we need to roll up our sleeves and determine how to change the core processes that govern an organization. The work in this chapter, while perhaps the most serious and detailed, is absolutely necessary if we are to get at the heart of the *Insider's Rule Book* and rewrite it.

Setting Goals

We break goal setting into six key steps:

1. Gain consensus on what drives success.

2. Identify critical processes.

3. Determine measures for drivers of success and key processes.

4. Complete an environmental scan.

5. Establish point-of-arrival goals.

6. Establish the next year's goals.

Step 1. Gain Consensus on What Drives Success

Before you can set any goals, you need to be clear about what you should be setting goals for. Sure, you could set a goal of reducing tardiness by 10 percent, but will it matter in the end? Probably not. That was an easy one to answer. The harder question is, What *will* matter in achieving your company's vision?

Certainly goals that relate to what drives your company's success in achieving its vision should matter most. The first step, then, is to determine those drivers of success in the business, or what you need to focus on to achieve that vision. John Menzer, as chief financial officer (CFO) of Wal-Mart, credited this basic idea for helping to kick the company in the pants and, after a long period of uninspiring performance, to refocus on profitable growth.

A company's management can get so distracted by putting out fires every day that it fails to stop and ask provocative questions, but it needs to. Even more important, it needs to take the time to answer it collectively.

This step requires that your senior management team block a day to determine what particular things drive success in the business, the ones that the organization needs to focus on to achieve its vision. Coming up with a laundry list will be easy; prioritizing the items into the top drivers will not.

First, of course, you need to review the company's vision statement. This document outlines what's really important to the company. Remember that eventually you will be setting goals, and those goals should support achieving that vision.

Use the Post-it process described in chapter 6 to identify and classify the goals. Following the driver diagram process, also from chapter 6, prioritize the Post-its, winnowing them down to the top three to six drivers of success. You don't want a laundry list. Once again what produces value is the process itself—the give-and-take, the open discussion, and the consensus building.

To determine how people want to prioritize the drivers, try the $100 test. Tell the participants they each have an imaginary $100 to spend any way they want on the drivers of success. Chances are that during the previous discussions, especially during the driver diagram exercise, everyone got a clear sense of what the company's most important drivers of success are—the ones that have the most dramatic impact on achieving the vision. Here they can cast their "vote" with their wallets.

When everyone is done voting, add up the total spent on each driver of success. You'll quickly reveal the group's priorities. For illustrative purposes, the final product might look something like figure 8-3.

I've seen this exercise work in Internet start-ups, steel refineries, hospitals, fast-food companies, and you name it. It works because it forces people to think about the business as a business, not just as a collection of departments or functions. It also depoliticizes this strategic discussion, because instead of focusing on individual targets and responsibilities, it highlights what the *organization as a whole* needs to do successfully to achieve its vision.

Step 2. Identify Critical Processes
Identifying your company's drivers of success is a major part of establishing the key measures for which the company will set its goals; but you're not done. You also need to examine what the critical processes for achieving the associated goals are.

You need to do this for two reasons. First, you want to establish goals that everyone in the organization can participate in achieving. Not everyone, especially at the lower levels, will be able to relate what they do to the drivers of success, but they should be able to relate their jobs to the critical processes you identify. Second, your drivers of success can be influenced by critical processes in the company, and you need to understand these relationships. For example, innovation—one driver of success—might be impacted by the company's product development process. If your company is to succeed overall, the people need to understand and improve both its drivers of success as well as its critical processes.

FIGURE 8-3
Sample Results of the $100 Test

DRIVER OF SUCCESS	TEAM MEMBER A	TEAM MEMBER B	OTHERS	TOTAL	PRIORITY RANKING
A	$80	$70	⟶	$300	1
B			⟶	$200	2
C		$10	⟶	$100	3
D	$10		⟶	$50	4
E	$10	$20	⟶	$50	5

To complete this step, your team will need to go through a similar set of exercises that was used to identify the drivers of success. First, gather your team to brainstorm what the critical processes are that your company depends on, the ones that in essence run the business. Once you've identified them, the team needs to group them into categories to see the "big picture." Finally, prioritize the handful of critical processes, using such tools as the driver diagram and the $100 test. In identifying the priorities, examine the relationships between the critical processes and the company's drivers of success as well.

Without knowing your company, it is impossible to predict what your critical processes will be. Some examples of what other companies have come up with are exhibited in figure 8-4.

Step 3. Determine Measures for Drivers of Success and Key Processes

To set measurable goals, you first need to identify the measures themselves. You have a head start, having figured out what your drivers of success and critical processes are, but that's not enough.

You might have identified innovation as a driver of success, but how are you going to measure that? Unless you define a clear measure, you can't set a specific goal for it, which is your ultimate objective.

Your team needs to brainstorm alternative measures for each driver of success and critical process and then select the most viable one for each. There is no easy way to conduct this activity other than to come together as a group and have everyone put her best ideas forward. To get the ball rolling, see figure 8-5 for examples from other companies.

I suggest you let a small group of people develop these measures first. Then have other groups in the organization confirm their choices or come up with something better. The point is that because everyone will have to

FIGURE 8-4
Sample Critical Processes

New Product Development	Editorial Creation	Product Testing
Creative Development	Order Entry	Billing and Collection
Order Picking and Delivery	Materials Handling	Research and Development

FIGURE 8-5
Alternative Measures for Success Drivers

DRIVER OF SUCCESS OR CRITICAL PROCESS	MEASURE
On-time delivery	Percent of shipments that are on time
Innovation	Percent of sales coming from products introduced in the last two years
Customer satisfaction	Index score on a customer satisfaction survey
Customer loyalty	(Total customers − lost customers)/number of customers
New product development	Product development cycle time
Product quality	Percent defects
Employee satisfaction	Score on an annual attitude survey

abide by these measures, they need to be widely understood and accepted as "the right ones" to use.

Step 4. Complete an Environmental Scan

Imagine for a moment that you're a member of a sports team, and I present you with a simple bet. The terms are that if you put up $100 and your side wins, you'll get $300. If your side loses, however, you lose the $100. Assuming this gambling was all legal, would you take the bet?

At the moment, anyway, you simply don't have enough information to take the bet, do you? All you know is that you are a member of a team, but you still don't know enough about the circumstances to determine whether it's a good bet. It could be a slam dunk, the easiest money you've ever made. Then again, you could be kissing $100 good-bye.

You might agree to this bet if you've beaten the opposing team eight times before; but then again, you'd still have questions. Do you have all the same players as the other eight times you faced the other team? Do they have the same lineup? Did you last play them a month ago or five years ago? Even more basic, just what kind of game are you playing any-way—soccer? Water polo? You'd surely want those important answers before taking the bet.

It's amazing how often a company will take a bet, or go into goal setting and resource allocation—also known as budgeting—without everyone meeting first to understand the current operating environment. It's like the story of the blindfolded people who gathered around an elephant. Each could only feel one part, so each came to a different conclusion about what type of animal they were touching. The man who felt the trunk cried out, "It's a python!" But the man who felt the tail said, "No, it's not. It's a lion!"

In most companies, especially large ones (although I've seen it in organizations with less than twenty-five people), everyone is charged with different responsibilities, or pieces of the elephant, and, as a result, has different perspectives of the company. You'll find the problem with the goal-setting process is that nothing about it brings all employees together to compare notes and "see" the entire beast. And without this connection, you can't have a shared understanding or meeting of the minds.

Thus, you need to engage your company in an environmental scan. This type of meeting serves three purposes. It increases the shared knowledge of the current situation by bringing together different views or perspectives. Next, it provides managers with a better understanding of the current situation, which will enable them to "place bets" with some knowledge. Finally, it gets everyone focused, creating a consensus that will provide the foundation to establish goals.

The vehicle for an environmental scan is typically a two-day retreat, with a great deal of preparation beforehand. Tailor your agenda to your company's needs. It might include, for example, reviews of the following elements:

- The organization's vision and values

- Its performance versus last year's plan

- Customer satisfaction surveys

- Performance of key drivers, if previously developed

- Execution of critical processes, if previously developed

- Key competitor performance against that of the company

- Employee feedback

- Strengths, weaknesses, opportunities, and threats

In addition, you might also pose a list of key questions that each business unit needs to answer and discuss with the management gathered at the retreat. Such questions might cover:

- What has surprised you most about the business during the past year? How did you respond to it?

- What are the five things you are most worried about and why?

- What are the five things you are most excited about and why?

- What one thing would you change about the business today if you could?

- What channels of distribution need to be expanded or changed?

- What's the most significant consumer trend you're aware of relating to your business?

- Which core competencies need to be strengthened? Why?

Now some individuals in your company might feel that they are constantly looking at all of these issues. That might be true, but the point here is to bring everyone together to review them at the same time and form a consensus on what they see. You just might hear, "By Jove, it's an elephant!"

After going through the process of an environmental scan, your company should also know what a reasonable bet is and be in a position to start establishing its goals.

Step 5. Establish Point-of-Arrival Goals

A point-of-arrival goal is *a numerical target that indicates the best your company thinks it can possibly do on any specific measure*. Perhaps its goal is one defect out of 1 million products sold or operating costs at 5 percent of revenue.

There is intentional flexibility in this term. We might think it will take three years before a company can achieve perfection in one measure, while another might take five years. The point isn't quite so much *when* it'll reach a certain target but *what* that target should be.

Using the foundation of the environmental scan and all that you learned from it, your senior management team should be able to put a stake in the ground. In essence, they're saying, "Given all that we know about ourselves, our competition, and our market, this target is what we should be aiming to achieve long term with this particular measure."

No magic formula exists for establishing these point-of-arrival goals; it requires some judgment. *Judgment*, you're thinking, *isn't that just as political as what we had before?*

The difference is that you've built a companywide consensus based on facts and experience. This situation isn't at all what the company had before. In the past, divisions or business units would offer some sanitized view of the world, presenting only what put them in a good light. They'd urge, "We should take the bet. We've beaten this team eight times before, and now we have home field advantage! We have a slight problem with our quarterback, but it's nothing we can't work around."

The new process forces businesspeople to discuss a wide range of highly pertinent topics, yielding a complete and well-informed view for *everyone* who participates. "Okay," they'll admit, "our record this year stinks, at no wins and five losses, and our competition has won every game they've played this year. And yes, our starting quarterback is out for the season. But we have a fighting chance!"

The rules have changed. It's all about evidence and argument. Now with all the information out on the table—complete transparency if you will—nobody wants to risk looking bad by pushing an indefensible point of view. You'll need to gather your facts and present a coherent argument if you want to get support, for anything less will make you look ill prepared or worse.

What is in your company's best interest now is for you to study the facts and really get to know your market and competitors so that you can win support for your ideas. This move is *exactly* what your shareholders want you to do, and now it's in your best interest to pursue it, too.

After the long-term point-of-arrival goals are set, you will need to document them and communicate them to the people in your organization. See figure 8-6 for an example of how you might do that.

Notice in this illustration that the point-of-arrival goal for customer loyalty is just 85 percent. While that target might seem low, the industry

FIGURE 8-6
Communicating the Point-of-Arrival Goals

DRIVER OF SUCCESS OR CRITICAL PROCESS	MEASURE	CURRENT MEASURE	POINT OF ARRIVAL GOAL
On-time delivery	Percent of shipments that are on time	80%	99.5%
Innovation	Percent of sales coming from products introduced in the last two years	30%	60%
Customer satisfaction	Index score on a customer satisfaction survey	80	95
Customer loyalty	(Total customers − lost customers)/number of customers	55%	85%
New product development	Product development cycle time	2 years	6 months
Product quality	Percent defects	2%	0.1%
Employee satisfaction	Score on an annual attitude survey	87	95

average was 55 percent and the industry leader was estimated at 90 percent. Management here decided that given the investment dollars it would have to expend on customer loyalty programs to meet or beat the industry leader, the investment would simply not pay off. It recognized the industry leader had the first-mover advantage. Yet management felt that investing enough to move up to 85 percent from the industry average of 55 percent would increase profitability and shareholder value.

Also in figure 8-6, the point-of-arrival goal for employee satisfaction is a score of 95 points on an annual attitude survey, while the current score is 87 points. That might not sound like a much of a stretch; however, employee satisfaction was a high priority for this sample company for the previous three years, when many innovative programs were successfully introduced. While management there feels that more could be done, its point-of-arrival goal takes into account the hard work and progress that has already been made.

To recap, the leadership of your company has met and defined what drives success in the business (or for each specific business unit if it's a large company) and what the critical processes are. Then it took the time to create a specific measure for each driver and critical process. Next, management developed a well-informed consensus view of the company's current environment, enough to establish point-of-arrival goals for each measure.

If done well and properly, the entire process you have witnessed so far has been an intellectual and business exercise grounded in fact, informed debate, and collective experience. There hasn't been room for political maneuvering, and there'd be little purpose served in doing so. People might still try such tactics, but they'll make themselves painfully transparent (and learn quickly that it's no longer how the game is won).

All of your work—and you've accomplished a great deal—has been done in preparation of setting annual goals.

Step 6. Establish the Next Year's Goals

In this step, you'll see how all of your time invested pays off. You've done so much to build a companywide consensus that at this point many of the answers to the question of establishing the next year's goals should be evident.

Again, taking measures from figure 8-6, customer loyalty currently stands at 55 percent, the industry average, and the point-of-arrival goal is set at 85 percent. Your people have a shared understanding of why the company sits at 55 percent and why it has selected 85 percent as its ultimate goal. They've talked about what drives customer loyalty and what other companies are doing about it. In short, they know their stuff. More important, everyone shares that understanding.

Now the only question is what progress you should make on this goal for next year. Should you shoot for boosting your loyalty measures or just try to hold your own? Given what you've learned about the competition and what they're up to and given your past success with customer loyalty promotions, 60 percent is a reasonable stretch target for a one-year effort.

Once again, this consensus view is based on hard-gathered, fact-based analysis. If people want to argue, they will need to argue facts, not personalities.

Now let's turn to employee satisfaction. Your last score on the employee survey was 87 points, and in the long term you want to stand at 95 points. Once again, should you strive to make progress here, or hold your own next year?

You need to consider outside influences when making these decisions, too. When reviewing the competition, for example, it turns out that your salespeople heard that a key competitor is hiring and would most likely try to "steal" some of your employees. While other priorities might have overshadowed employee satisfaction because management was somewhat complacent, this news reinforces the need to make progress. On average, management decides to look for a two-point improvement on the survey, from 87 points to 89 points in the next year.

We could go on, but I think you see the process at this point. It's based on three principles—shared understanding, consensus, and judgment. The shared understanding is necessary to provide the basis for sound judgment and to create consensus, and you can't reach consensus without reasoned judgment. Taken together, they produce an entirely new rule book for establishing goals.

Planning

Now that your company has set long-term, point-of-arrival goals, as well as one-year goals for all of its key measures, it's time to figure out exactly how to achieve them. Most likely you've already discussed some of that when developing those goals, but now you need to make a plan.

In some respects, what the company has done so far has already redefined the former planning process. Instead of senior management soliciting plans from the various functional areas or divisions, it first defines the company's key measurable goals for the next year and then asks its divisions to outline what they can do to support achieving these goals.

But management needs to do more; otherwise, the company will still see too much horse trading (less of it, for sure, but it will still happen). The company therefore needs to establish a system that will encourage people in each layer of the organization to think about what role they have in supporting the company's goals and then to build a plan accordingly.

In the nonpolitical workplace, there are five steps to approach planning:

1. Identify the primary owner of each key goal.

2. Identify strategic initiatives to meet each goal.

3. Cascade projects and goals.

4. Build the game plan.

5. Allocate resources.

Step 1. Identify the Primary Owner of Each Key Goal

To provide the necessary leadership to achieve each stated goal, someone from your senior management team needs to assume ownership. This person will spearhead your company's effort to achieve the annual goal and will serve as the overall project manager and coordinator.

She won't be out there on her own, however; she'll lead a team of people dedicated to achieving your company's important goal. Everyone on her team will have a personal incentive to reach the goal (discussed later), as will your entire senior management team, so she'll get the support that she needs.

The primary owner's first task is to form a project team. She will choose individuals representing areas that have a major role to play in the success of meeting the stated goal. It's best to have a three- to eight-person team to keep it manageable. Many other people will be involved later on in the process, so for now she needs a relatively small group.

The primary owner's next job, shared with her teammates, is to develop strategic initiatives to meet your company's stated goal. She must then ensure that these initiatives are implemented (as detailed later in this chapter).

One question remains: Who should be the overall "grand marshal" of all the goals identified? To whom should the primary owners for each goal report? In most organizations, that person is your CEO. It's ultimately her job to do everything possible to achieve the goals the company has set forth. If specific goals are not met—for whatever reason, including turf battles and other political positioning—she must weigh in and make the necessary decisions to get everyone back on track.

Building on our earlier example, figure 8-7 shows how the ownership of each goal breaks out in the company.

In this case, the project team consists of people from various departments and not just from the function represented by the primary owner. This arrangement, with its cross-functional commitment and cooperation, ensures that the team will achieve its important goals. That cooperation is much easier to obtain when the department from which it needs help is already represented on the team (and doubly so when the people involved have personal rewards tied to the team's success).

FIGURE 8-7
Ownership of Goals

DRIVER OF SUCCESS OR CRITICAL PROCESS	MEASURE	PRIMARY OWNER	TEAM COMPOSITION
On-time delivery	Percent of shipments that are on time	Tom S. (VP logistics)	Logistics, operations
Innovation	Percent of sales coming from products introduced in the last two years	Susan S. (VP marketing)	Marketing, new product development
Customer satisfaction	Index score on a customer satisfaction survey	William K. (CFO)	Market research, finance, marketing
Customer loyalty	(Total customers − lost customers)/ number of customers	George H. (VP sales)	Sales, marketing, finance
New product development	Product development cycle time	Elizabeth M. (VP new product development)	New product development, operations, sales
Product quality	Percent defects	Brian G. (VP operations)	Operations, marketing
Employee satisfaction	Score on an annual attitude survey	Stanley K. (VP human resources)	Human resources, functional heads

Step 2. Identify Strategic Initiatives to Meet Each Goal

Once the project team convenes and all of it members are fully briefed, it needs to examine what drives the measure it's evaluating and then brainstorm alternative solutions for reaching that goal. After they are defined, they refer to the solutions as strategic initiatives. Here's a simple process that the project team can follow:

- Define rules for the brainstorming session: No personal criticism, no one person dominates the discussion, build on the ideas of others, be creative, everyone participates, and keep the discussion moving.

- Clarify the specific measure and goal that the team is trying to achieve, and allow a couple of minutes for people to gather their thoughts.

- Ask members to let their ideas flow. Go around the room and ask everyone to contribute one idea.

- Record the ideas as they are generated. Don't discuss them, and keep the session moving.

- Go through as many rounds as appropriate. When no one proposes any more ideas, discuss each brainstormed idea so that it's fully developed and consistently understood. Combine similar ideas.

- Prioritize the best possible ideas.

A tool that can help the team prioritize the best solutions is called a decision grid. First, the group decides the key criteria on which it will judge each idea—for example, cost effectiveness, meets customer needs, and speed to implement. Then the group evaluates each idea using some type of scoring—that is, 1 = does not meet criteria, 2 = somewhat meets criteria, and 3 = good at meeting criteria. When the team adds up all the individual scores, the ones with the most points are the team's priority projects.

Figure 8-8 is an example of what a completed decision grid might look like, assuming a team of three people.

FIGURE 8-8
Sample Decision Grid

Assumes a team of three people

	COST EFFECTIVE	MEETS CUSTOMER NEEDS	SPEED TO IMPLEMENT	TOTALS PER SOLUTION	PRIORITY RANK
Solution A	$1+1+1=3$	$1+2+2=5$	$1+1+1=3$	11	3
Solution B	$2+3+2=7$	$1+2+3=6$	$3+3+2=8$	21	1
Solution C	$1+2+2=5$	$1+1+1=3$	$1+2+3=6$	14	2

The team can make this tool more sophisticated by assigning a weight to each of the criteria. Then some criteria will count comparatively more than others.

Assume for the moment that we are part of the project team tasked with finding solutions to increase employee satisfaction, and our goal is to increase the score on the annual survey from 87 points to 89 points, as established by the senior management team during the goal-setting phase. After much brainstorming, we have a list of possible solutions. Using the decision grid, we determine our top four solutions. Given that we only have a year, we really need to focus our efforts.

Here's what we've decided. We're going to establish ongoing employee dialogue to keep workers well informed, to improve understanding of employee pay and benefits, to create more job autonomy, and generally to improve employee communication.

To see this process more clearly, review the tree diagram in figure 8-9. This diagram outlines all of the initiatives the team recommends.

For each of the separate initiatives, the team also needs to assign a specific measure and goal. As an example, the team could measure improving employee communications with a score from an employee survey, and the goal might be to score four out of a possible five marks. The point is that each strategic initiative needs a clear, measurable definition of success.

While developing strategic initiatives is a vital first step, the process doesn't end there. The project team needs to translate them into actions if these initiatives are to be effective.

FIGURE 8-9
Tree Diagram of Possible Solutions

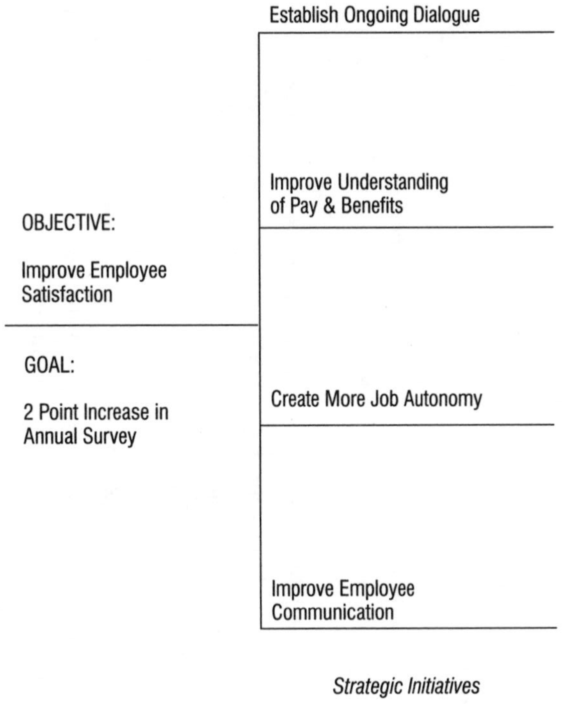

Establish Ongoing Dialogue

Improve Understanding
of Pay & Benefits

Create More Job Autonomy

OBJECTIVE:

Improve Employee
Satisfaction

GOAL:

2 Point Increase in
Annual Survey

Improve Employee
Communication

Strategic Initiatives

Have you ever heard the riddle of the three frogs sitting on a log? One decides to jump into the pond. Now how many frogs are on the log? Any guesses? The right answer is three. There are still three frogs on the log because the frog that decided to jump hasn't done it yet.

Deciding to do something and actually doing it are two different things. Many companies stop at the point of having decided to create more job autonomy or to improve employee communications. Without mechanisms to make those initiatives happen, the goals they are supposed to fulfill—as indeed the whole process—are undermined. If the team fails to enlist people's help in achieving those goals, this inaction often results in the leadership vacuum that office politics rushes in to fill. So performance can again boil down to paying lip service to a handful of goals, while energies are reconverted into fiefdom building and masterminding.

To avoid this mistake, we'll need to cascade the projects down through the organization. But how?

Step 3. Cascade Projects and Goals

Each team member now needs to take primary ownership of one or more strategic initiative. The senior person who led this effort to develop the strategic initiatives now assumes the role of the grand marshal, overseeing the work done by each of her teams and providing them with the necessary support to be successful.

The next step is for each strategic initiative owner to recruit members to his team and hold a kick-off meeting to outline their objective and goals. Then the team needs to brainstorm possible solutions, prioritize them, and select the three or so of the most promising ideas. Is this process beginning to sound familiar? Good, it should. The process of cascading goals and objectives down through the organization relies on the same simple mechanisms that created the strategic initiatives. That simple but highly effective approach ensures consistency and goal alignment and clearly delineates people's roles in this effort.

Assuming now that each team has identified its projects in support of the strategic initiatives, they can all be captured in a single tree diagram (see figure 8-10).

What comes next? Each person on the team that developed the supporting projects becomes a primary owner of one or more of these proj-

FIGURE 8-10
Tree Diagram of Cascading Projects

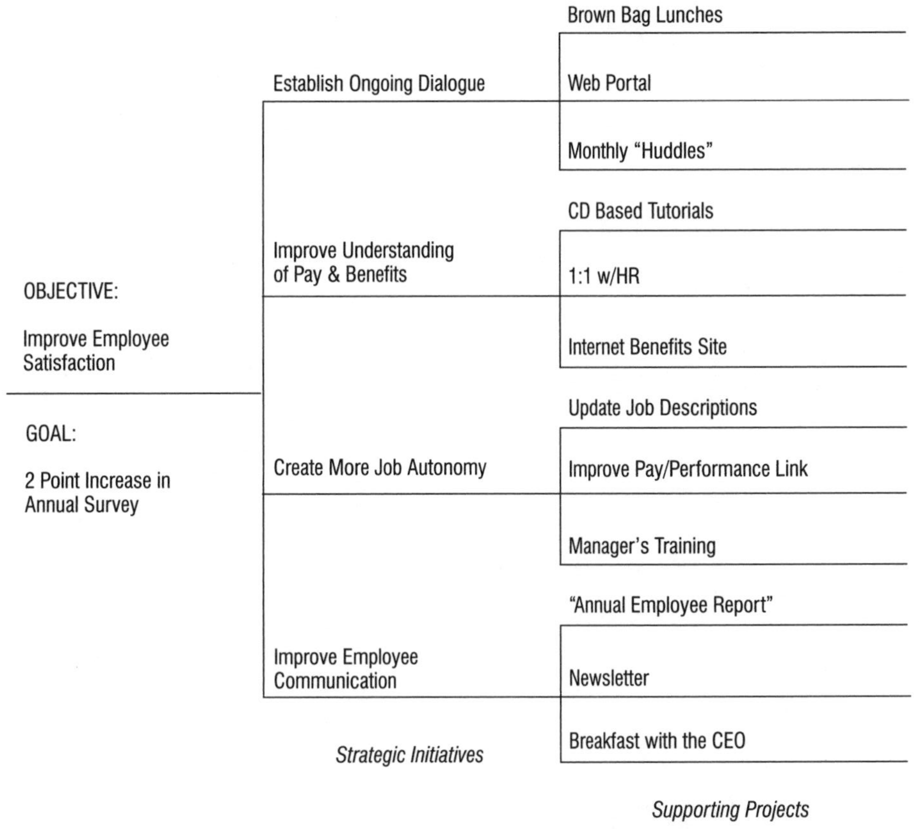

OBJECTIVE:
Improve Employee Satisfaction

GOAL:
2 Point Increase in Annual Survey

- Establish Ongoing Dialogue
  - Brown Bag Lunches
  - Web Portal
  - Monthly "Huddles"
- Improve Understanding of Pay & Benefits
  - CD Based Tutorials
  - 1:1 w/HR
  - Internet Benefits Site
- Create More Job Autonomy
  - Update Job Descriptions
  - Improve Pay/Performance Link
  - Manager's Training
- Improve Employee Communication
  - "Annual Employee Report"
  - Newsletter
  - Breakfast with the CEO

Strategic Initiatives   *Supporting Projects*

ects, forms a project team, and breaks the projects down even further. The process ends when we get to a task level, or when we have tactical details, as illustrated in figure 8-11.

Once this procedure is complete, everyone connected with these strategic initiatives, supporting projects, or tactics (which will obviously be a large percentage of the workforce) can squarely answer the question, What's my role in this? Everyone else will learn their roles when the plan is developed, which is our next topic.

Step 4. Build the Game Plan

Okay, the project teams have set their goals and defined the initiatives to meet them. Not every worker is on a project team, but every worker needs to know what the goals are and what his role is in achieving them. The company's game plan needs to lay out for all workers what they should be doing both in support of specific projects, if applicable, and in their daily jobs to ensure the organization meets its overall goals. The game plan also needs to establish milestones that workers can use as guides throughout the year to track their progress. If they know how they're doing at all times, they can make course adjustments as necessary.

It all sounds good in theory, but what's the mechanism to make this game plan work? First, managers develop role profiles for each of their employees. A role profile defines a person's role within the organization in terms of its purpose and a set of expected capabilities. It contains all of the same information that's commonly found in a standard job description, only it goes a step further in explaining the purpose of the job as it fits into the department and the organization as a whole. In addition, it details both the qualifications for the job and the key capabilities that will make the candidate successful. Specifically, the role profile explains at what competency level the candidate should be performing for each of the leadership characteristics the company has defined (in the process described in chapter 7). The role profile requires more detail than a typical job description, but it is a rich document that reinforces the work the company has done in defining its desired leadership characteristics.

Next, the company identifies key results areas (KRAs) for each worker's role in the organization. These simple, short phrases—headlines, if you will—clarify the jobholder's responsibilities in meeting the organiza-

FIGURE 8-11
Tactical Level Goals

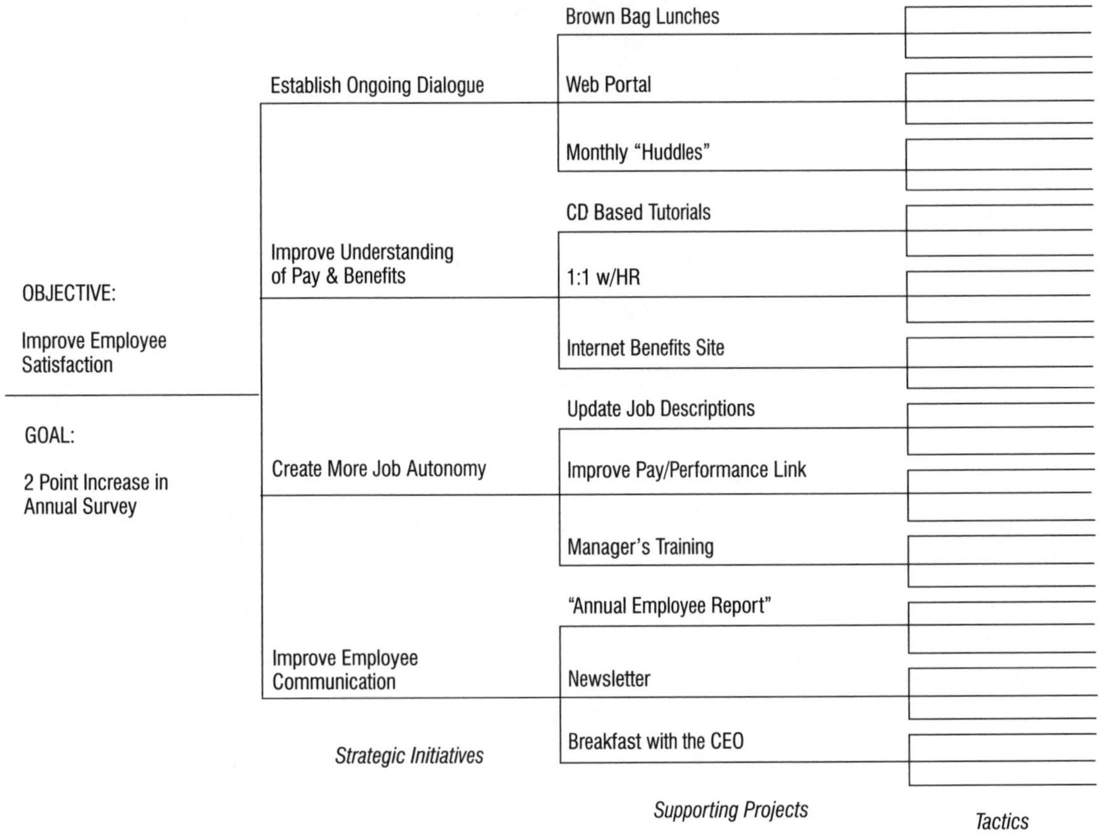

OBJECTIVE:

Improve Employee Satisfaction

GOAL:

2 Point Increase in Annual Survey

Improve Employee Communication

Establish Ongoing Dialogue

Improve Understanding of Pay & Benefits

Create More Job Autonomy

Brown Bag Lunches

Web Portal

Monthly "Huddles"

CD Based Tutorials

1:1 w/HR

Internet Benefits Site

Update Job Descriptions

Improve Pay/Performance Link

Manager's Training

"Annual Employee Report"

Newsletter

Breakfast with the CEO

Strategic Initiatives

Supporting Projects

Tactics

tion's goals. They are derived from an examination of the company's goals and the role that the results area plays in supporting them, including any involvement on project teams. In addition, a general understanding of how the worker's role can contribute to the organization's success should be considered in developing the KRAs. An example for an HR manager might be:

- To deliver and develop the right people, in the right place, at the right time

- To translate the company's values into actionable and measurable behaviors

- To deliver information systems and supporting processes to enable on-line individual performance assessment

Companies also use goal sheets to ensure both goal alignment and achievement. Here high-level statements concerning a worker's KRAs get translated into something more tangible for planning purposes. (We'll explore goal sheets in depth in chapter 9.)

The next step in this process is to establish specific, measurable, attainable, results-oriented, time-bound (SMART) objectives for each KRA. If the worker is a member of a project team, then his SMART objectives are set within that context.

The company then develops milestones, or the major steps that workers need to execute to meet an objective. In essence, they are formalized to-do lists to keep things on track and to inform the manager's boss of the steps needed to meet the company's objectives.

Finally, management schedules performance updates based on the milestones of each SMART objective.

At this point we need to revisit the initiatives and SMART objectives for each area and at each level. Do we have proper consistency, alignment, and commitment? Are all of our efforts, or the arrows, pointed in the same direction? If we do everything we say we want to do, will we achieve all that we need to this year? We might find areas that need fine-tuning, but it should be evident where and to what degree.

The only question now is, Can we do it all? That's where management's decisions regarding resource allocation step in to finalize the process.

Step 5. Allocate Resources

You might not have thought of it in these terms before, but how your company allocates its resources—people, money, and time—in any given year governs what it does in that year. Senior management might say that expanding into the Northeast is important to do this year, but if only an imperceptible part of the budget is dedicated to it and salespeople are told to call on old customers, not new ones, chances are the company will not see any expansion into the Northeast after all.

To avoid this scenario, we need to integrate our work of developing goals and initiatives thus far into the actual process of allocating resources. Ignoring this core process or assuming this integration will happen naturally is a big mistake, one that many companies have made. All the exciting goals and projects that people have worked so hard to develop will fade away (and spur cynicism) if they don't get the resources they require to realize their goals.

The process of allocating resources is most commonly known as budgeting, or annual planning. *Oh, that*, you're thinking. While the process is not often perceived as governing what a company does, when you strip it down, it does dictate what program gets funded and what doesn't.

Ask anyone how political the budgeting process is within his or her company, and you're likely to hear, "Are you kidding?" According to a February 1998 survey of *CFO Magazine* readers, the budget process is driven more by politics than by strategy in 75 percent of the companies that participated.[1] Does the enemy within threaten to rear its head at this point in our process, too?

Thankfully, we've already done an immense amount of work in preparation for this moment. The typical budgeting process involves simply throwing meat (resources) to the lions and waiting to see which ones dominate. Uninspired department heads will fight over resources to protect their turf, and the more determined ones will fight to expand their empires. What we have done, however, is establish both a clear set of organizational goals in support of the company's shared vision and an objective criterion for evaluating our resource requests.

In the nonpolitical workplace, ambitious leaders will still strive for power; but here they will channel their ambition to serve the higher interests of the organization.

Usually, the finance department facilitates the allocation process, and that's true in a nonpolitical workplace as well. The finance people work with the managers to develop their funding requirements for their projects as well as their ongoing staffing budgets. They also work with the marketing and other department heads to translate their established goals into financial terms and produce documents, such as a projected profit and loss statement, to communicate the financial results of all the various planned activities.

The senior management team reviews these documents and determines if the final results meet all of the firm's guiding goals and objectives, including the financial targets. If they are not being met, the senior management team will work with the various initiative leaders and department heads to review alternatives. The objective criterion is, What most clearly and effectively supports the achievement of our shared vision and our measurable goals?

When management determines the planned programs and levels of spending are sufficient to meet the firm's overall goals, it "blesses" the budget. Then the resource allocation process is concluded.

At this point for every manager in the organization, we've been able to answer clearly two questions: What needs to be accomplished? And what's my role in that? We need to answer as well the last crucial question, What's in it for me? That's the subject of the next chapter.

Notes

1   "21st Century Planning," *CFO Magazine,* (Feb. 1998), 30.

CHAPTER 9

Establishing New Criteria for Rewards
What's in It for Me?

The deepest urge in human nature is the desire to be impor-tant. —JOHN DEWEY

At this point, we seem to have it all. We have a shared vision, a con-crete course of action, and workers who know their role in getting it all done. Frankly, that's more than what most organizations have, but it's still not enough to reform a political organization and create a single unified team. We need to align *all* the reward systems as well.

Many people are deeply motivated when they genuinely feel part of something larger than themselves, the feeling our process engenders. I once worked with a CEO of a large publishing and direct-mail house who thought he understood this powerful source of motivation. He kicked off one quarterly meeting with all of his managers by announcing, "You are part of something larger than yourselves, you're part of [company name]." He couldn't understand why he didn't see a sizable increase in commitment. Hadn't he used the right words?

While I believe that creating this collective sense of purpose that

154

bonds every worker to the organization's greater good is vital, it's not enough. From the beginning of this book, I've emphasized that in order to reform office politics, individuals' self-interests must be aligned with the organization's interests. The stronger this alignment, the greater the likelihood that people will act in the organization's best interests and that is our ultimate aim.

Having clearly defined what those organizational interests are—through creating a shared vision, values, measures, and goals—showing workers their roles in supporting those interests is absolutely critical. After all, we can't align their individual interests with organizational interests if we don't know what those interests are, right? If the organization does not *consistently* reward its people for acting in the organization's best interests, however, they'll become confused. This confusion has the potential to unravel all that we've accomplished so far.

In this chapter, we'll describe how an organization should align its reward systems and the various (simple) tools it can use to do so. This final step ensures that every worker can answer all three vital questions we've posed: What needs to be accomplished? What's my role in that? And what's in it for me? Having answered all of these questions, we will have completely rewritten the *Insider's Rule Book* and, in so doing, filled the leadership void that first gave rise to the political workplace.

Goal Sheets

One of the most effective tools available in a company's reward system, and surprisingly one of the easiest to implement, is a goal sheet. It describes each individual's goals for the upcoming year, the measures for judging success, and the reward for achieving each goal.

The goal sheet's design is easy enough, but what integrates it into all the work we've done so far and makes it so effective is the process by which the goal sheets are completed. First, let's look at an example of a goal sheet (see figure 9-1).

Goals stem from two sources. The first results from participating in a project team, in which case the goal reflects that individual's specific tasks for that team. The second comes from the SMART objectives developed in support of that person's key results areas (KRAs), as discussed in chap-

FIGURE 9-1
NuCo Company Goal Sheet

Employee's Name: John Doe

Manager's Name: Jane Smith

Date: _____

(Initial) Approved	(Initial) Approved

Goal Weighting: [0-100%] 40

1 Identify Your Goal "Headline"

Develop "brown-bag-lunch program"

2 Identify the Goal Chain (e.g., how this goal relates to Strategic Initiatives and/or Key Results Areas)

Brown-bag-lunch> establish ongoing employee dialogue> improve employee satisfaction

Also supports KRA "to deliver and develop the right people, in the right place, at the right time"

3 Identify Measures of Success

85% of participants rate the program as being "Very Valuable" in post session evaluation form

4 What Are Important Linkages (e.g., other groups, departments, projects impacted)

Division managers
Corporate communications

5 Tasks to Achieve Goal

Form project team
Identify and recruit members
Create a project plan
Establish milestones
Roll Out

6 Key Capabilities Required

Constructive collaboration
Driving results

7 Goal Results (Against Measures)

Goal Rating (Against Goal/Tasks): _____

ter 8. In some cases these two sources directly overlap—for example, when a project team member fulfills one of her KRAs through her team participation.

When filling out a goal sheet, the employee first puts his goal into a simple and direct "headline," one that captures the essence of what needs to be achieved. Second, he considers how this goal fits into and supports larger objectives. This goal chain makes explicit his contribution to the larger goals of the enterprise.

In step 3, he defines his specific measures of success, so that his performance can be judged objectively. The fourth step identifies important links to other projects or departments, essentially any that are materially impacted by his job. This part is important because it highlights where communication and collaboration are most required.

In step 5, the employee describes how he will achieve his goal. He'll have to consider the major activities and tasks he'll need to undertake and their order.

Step 6 ties back to the leadership appraisal form. In chapter 7 we identified the desired characteristics and behaviors of employees. Here in step 6 that information is put to practical use as the employee assesses the leadership traits, and the degree of proficiency, that he will need to meet his goals successfully. Incidentally, this information will also become the basis for individual development plans, which are determined by assessing the employee's performance gap between the desired and actual leadership proficiency required to achieve each goal.

The seventh step occurs at the end of the year, when the employee assesses his performance and compares it to what his manager thinks. Since the aim is to establish objective criteria on which to judge the employee's performance, there should be little discrepancy between their two views. If they don't agree, then the employee's performance will be judged by an individual at the next level up—that is, the manager's manager.

Each goal is given a weighting, anywhere between 0 and 100 percent (see the upper left-hand corner of the goal sheet). This weighting is determined first in a discussion between the manager and her subordinate and then in a review by the manager's boss. The weighting reflects the goal's importance. If the employee has three goals, they might each be weighted equally (or 33 percent), or if one goal is more important than the others, it will receive a higher weighting.

This same process is used to determine how the employee will earn a specific proficiency rating (see chapter 7). Using John Doe's goal of developing a brown-bag lunch program (see figure 9-1), we know that if 85 percent of the participants rate the program as very valuable then John will meet expectations, or receive an L3 rating. But what if only 75 percent rate it that highly or, on the other extreme, if 95 percent do? The answer needs to be determined before the fact, not after. And to ensure objectivity and fairness, it should be a joint decision between the manager and her subordinate, with a review and concurrence by the manager's boss.

The 360-Degree Evaluation

We discussed 360-degree evaluations in detail in chapter 7. It's worthwhile mentioning the evaluation here because it's one of two primary tools companies use to assess performance and provide commensurate rewards.

Companies need to define the explicit leadership behaviors and traits they desire from their employees. They then need to describe these behaviors in enough detail so that they can judge individual performance against them.

Performance Reviews, Merit Increases, and Bonuses

I have purposely lumped these three common reward components together, because they should each be based on an individual's goal sheets and 360-degree evaluations. Having said that, let's look at exactly how each one of them is handled.

Performance reviews are normally somewhat confrontational and uncomfortable for the manager and subordinate alike for two reasons. The manager subjectively rather than objectively judges the employee's performance, and then both sides feel the need to marshal arguments to defend their position. Frankly, if the manager doesn't like a subordinate, he's probably going to give the employee a less-than-stellar review. We all know that a performance review is a bit of a personality contest, which makes the whole process disquieting for everyone. Even those people who do well report worrying that a new boss might see things quite differently.

Employees also normally experience a high degree of anxiety leading up to the review process. People wonder, *How does my boss think I'm doing? What's he going to focus on? How much will that one run-in I had with him at the beginning of the year cost me?* Nobody knows the answers to these questions except the boss, who presumably will share them during the performance review.

Charles Coonradt, author of *The Game of Work*, says that work is like bowling:

> *Except there's a guy called a supervisor who stands in front of the pins with a curtain. He can see the pins, but the bowler can't. The bowler throws the ball, hears something, and asks, "How'd I do?" The supervisor says, "Change your grip." The bowler rolls again and asks once more, "How'd I do?" The supervisor says, "Move your foot." The bowler does and rolls once more. "How am I doing?" he asks. "Don't worry about it. You've got a review coming up in six months. We'll let you know then."*[1]

Fortunately, the work that we have done so far can significantly alter these dynamics and lift the curtain. Let's examine how.

Performance reviews in the new world will be based on an individual's goal sheets. There, in black and white and determined in advance, an individual will find his goals for the upcoming year. Furthermore, the goals will have specific measures, and he has also agreed up front to how management will judge his performance (L1 through L5 proficiency assessments). The employee only has to go out and do the best job possible. Each employee will know exactly how he or she is doing (probably before anyone else does, for that matter) without having to guess or "read the boss's mood."

A performance update can be held at any time. It gives the employee and the manager a chance to assess progress and answer any questions, such as, Are milestones being met? Are the numbers moving in the right direction? What unexpected roadblocks or potholes have been encountered, and what's been done about them? Can the supervisor be of any help, and if so, how?

The annual performance review is a process of looking at where the measurements have come out, understanding why they came out that way, and what could have been done differently or what lessons were learned. Because progress is monitored all year by the employee and periodically by his boss, there should be little room for surprise. The manager finalizes the performance rating for each goal, applies the appropriate weightings to each, and calculates the final performance rating. The manager then reviews and discusses the final rating with her subordinate, as well as with her boss, and all three sign off on it.

Will the process work out this nicely and neatly 100 percent of the time? No, not likely. Isolated cases will require an extra dollop of judgment, but that's to be expected. These cases will be the exception and not the rule. When we compare where we were before—with the supervisor holding the curtain and the poor bowler struggling to perform—we've made real progress.

Okay, that's the performance review part of the equation. Now let's take a look at the second major component that will determine an individual's rewards.

In the new world the leadership appraisal, which is also based on the 360-degree survey, will be completed for every manager. Just how well each manager demonstrates the organization's values—be it in driving results, constructive collaboration, treating people with respect, or decisive action—will be determined by a survey of that manager's peers, subordinates, and superiors. Again, the scores will range from an L1 (exceeds expectations) to L5 (does not meet expectations), and the total score will be an average of all the individual components surveyed.

Each manager will wind up with two scores—one derived from the performance appraisal, which is based on the goal sheets, and the other from the leadership appraisal, which is based on the 360-degree survey. Each appraisal is designed to align an individual's best interests with that of the overall organization, which will reward him accordingly.

Specifically, merit increases will be based on the scores of an individual's performance appraisal and leadership appraisal. How much weight should be given to each one, and what the corresponding increase will be, will depend on the organization's circumstances. I have seen some companies refuse to award any merit increase when an individual scored the lowest possible, or an L5, on a performance appraisal; other companies weight both appraisals equally; and still others more heavily weight the leadership appraisal. It is important that the organization communicate its rules so that people can act in their own best interests.

Likewise, bonus payments, which are often restricted to higher-level managers, need to be tied to the scores on the performance and leadership appraisals. Here I have seen even wider deviations. While some companies offer token bonuses (think of the old Christmas bonus phenomenon), others double or triple a manager's salary. I'm not going to espouse any amount, but I'll simply advise on what the bonus should be based.

One common practice related to bonus payouts must change to make linking bonuses to performance and leadership appraisals effective. In a surprisingly large number of cases, companies wait until the end of the year, calculate what they can "afford" to pay out, and then back into the bonus formula. In these cases, the bonus has no real link to what an individual accomplished during the year.

That won't work here.

Now we will want to formalize what the bonus will be based on even before the year begins. Here's just one possible example. Let's say for simplicity that the scores on the leadership evaluation and the performance appraisal are weighted equally at 50 percent. A weighted average score of L3 (meets expectation) will pay out at 100 percent of the eligible bonus, and each level up or down will add or subtract 20 percent, respectively. The finance department could devise a budget for the bonus pool (perhaps keyed off of planned profitability or other means) that assumes everyone scores an L3 and gets 100 percent of their eligible bonus. If the average score is above that level, then, yes, the dollar amount will be higher, but the increased benefit to the organization should far outweigh the cost.

No matter what the bonus formula turns out to be, the most important determinant of success is clearly communicating expectations and measures well ahead of time. Then people will know what the rules are and how to act in their own best interests.

Linking Role Profiles and Leadership Appraisals

People care a great deal about their compensation and for good reason. Yet anyone with a modicum of ambition finds whatever it takes to move ahead just as important. *Sure I might get a little more in my wallet for playing along with these new rules,* you might be thinking, *but what will it take for me to get ahead? Has that really changed?*

A sure sign that the rules have really changed is when people notice a new group of up-and-comers. It might include some members of the old group; it might not. The new up-and-comers exhibit different behavior than the old class, and this new behavior is consistent with the company's stated values.

That behavior change might sound good, but it needs a mechanism to make it happen. Fortunately, there is a simple one that is amazingly effective—the role profiles introduced in chapter 8. The role profile details the qualifications for the job and the key capabilities that will make the candidate successful. Specifically, the role profile also designates at what level of competency the candidate should be performing for each of the leadership characteristics.

A worker who is eligible for a promotion would need first to demonstrate that he is performing at the required level for each leadership characteristic in the new position. In addition, there might be a requirement for a minimum rating on his most recent performance appraisal.

Should there be exceptions to this minimally acceptable rating for promotion? Perhaps, but management should thoughtfully challenge and then carefully communicate the rationale to avoid mixed signals. Each exception will diminish the company's credibility, so management needs to choose them wisely.

Other Rewards Not to Be Overlooked

So far we've covered material rewards, but we need to consider other rewards as well. Organization behaviorists (God bless 'em) call these psychic rewards, because they enhance people's psyches and make them feel better about themselves.

These rewards can be as subtle as a pat on the back or as obvious as a mention on the first page of the employee newsletter. They serve as public acknowledgements of a job well done.

Who is recognized in your company and for what reason? It's an important question, because workers are always aware of management's inconsistencies. Does the organization say it values one thing but publicly rewards another? While any one incident of perceived hypocrisy might be quickly dismissed and forgotten, if a pattern emerges, it can erode the people's faith in their leadership and in the other, material reward systems.

In chapter 7, I introduced the idea of an annual awards show to highlight top performers. Not only is this event fun, it loudly and clearly broadcasts just how committed the organization is to its stated values and performance goals. It also reinforces the idea that all rewards, even the psychic ones, are based on the same criteria and are inextricably linked.

Likewise, companies can coordinate and use their newsletters and web sites to reinforce the type of worker and achievement the organization desires. Although this effort requires a new level of cooperation from HR, corporate communications, and senior management, it's worth every hour spent.

Here's one last point about the connection between psychic and material rewards: This book's approach forces management to think through what it wants to accomplish, how it will go about achieving its goals, and what it needs from every employee. It's quite an eye-opening experience when management thoughtfully challenges what was once taken for granted and works to build a consensus view. In essence, the unofficial view of the world gets put right out in the open and is examined under a microscope. What develops is a fact-based view of the world, and the line between the "official" and the "unofficial" criteria for rewards disappears.

One consumer goods company used to assign profit-and-loss (P&L) responsibility to its product managers. Doing so was accepted industry practice, and it seemed that every product manager wanted to put that P&L responsibility on his résumé. Yet material rewards were only vaguely tied to bottom-line profitability.

The company tied all of its psychic rewards, however, to market share. All workers held their breath each month when the figures were released, and they speculated over them with the same ferocity as gamblers arguing over who will make the Final Four in the NCAA Championship. At the end of the day, product managers were only as good as their market shares.

What type of behavior do you think that engendered? As you might have guessed, every product manager focused on spending whatever was necessary to build market share. In a consumer goods company, that means offering deep discounts to the trade to stock its product in a desirable location, wildly outspending the competition on advertising, and sending out a blizzard of dollar-off coupons, just to name a few.

Is this strategy good for the company's bottom line? In theory, if it improves operating profit more than what it costs, yes. In practice, most of the time this market-share-at-any-cost strategy doesn't pay for itself. The company winds up only "renting" market share, which quickly snaps back to what it was before the spending flurry because customers' buying habits didn't really change. Much more often than not, the bottom line suffers. You might ask, "But didn't the product managers have 'P&L responsibility'? Shouldn't they care?"

What the product managers cared about was getting ahead, and although they indeed had P&L responsibility in theory, in practice it didn't really matter. If they wanted to earn their peers' respect and be considered an up-and-comer, they had to do whatever they could to boost market share.

When this same company decided to rewrite its *Insider's Rule Book,* the senior management team zeroed in on this problem. It assigned bottom-line profitability goals for product managers that dictated how merit increases and bonuses were paid out. It then wrote role profiles that spelled out the importance of building profitability along with brand awareness. Leadership appraisals also captured important elements of working with other departments, such as purchasing and operations, to improve the product's operating profit margin. The company's web site featured one product manager each month who embodied the essence of the company's values and desired leadership. In short, the difference in criteria between the material and psychic rewards disappeared.

The result? The market-share-at-any-cost mentality, so costly to the company and its shareholders, is dissolved.

Remember that organizations need to consider the psychic rewards and then integrate them into their material rewards programs to send out one unified and reinforcing message.

What It All Means

In this chapter, we have covered material rewards in the form of merit increases, bonuses, and promotions as well as psychic rewards. We've linked them ("stapled" might be a better word) to the other important components of our management system and, in doing so, have completely rewritten the *Insider's Rule Book*. In essence, we have made the *Official Rule Book* and the *Insider's Rule Book* one and the same. Now when people determine what is in their own best interests, or what will get them ahead, they'll also be acting in their organizations' best interests. They'll know what needs to be accomplished, what their role is in doing that, and what's in it for them.

We've created a system in which people who play by the rules win, people are rewarded based on merit, and people feel safe but not complacent. That system, my dear colleague, is your greatest competitive advantage.

Notes

1 John Case, *Open Book Management* (New York: HarperBusiness, 1996), 63–64.

CHAPTER 10

Personal Stories Revisited
It's a Whole New World

Sunlight is the best disinfectant.
—JUSTICE LOUIS DEMBITZ BRANDEIS

I n part I, you read personal stories about people who, while acting in their own best interests, became the enemy within. Some worked to undermine or even fire their colleagues, and others covered up important truths just to avoid upsetting important people.

The question now is, How likely, if at all, would their behavior change under the new *Insider's Rule Book?* What about the new system would discourage the destructive behavior they revealed?

Here, you'll have a chance to see the answers to those questions, not only from our perspective but actually from the people profiled. We sat down with them, walked them through the nonpolitical workplace, and asked them how they would have acted differently. Their answers will surprise you.

Karen's Story

CASE STUDY: A woman about to go on maternity leave is concerned that her job will be eliminated.

POLITICAL RESPONSE: She undermines the credibility of the person most likely to take her position.

What about the nonpolitical workplace that we described would have made a difference in Karen's story? First, let's take a quick look at some of the ways the *Insider's Rule Book* has changed (see figure 10-1). To begin with, Karen would have had well-defined goal sheets spelling out exactly what she needed to achieve. She would have understood her importance to the company, or her own value. She also would have seen that her own performance had nothing to do with whether someone else looked bad. Rather than focusing on the new guy, then, she would have best served her interests by working toward her own well-defined goals.

What about her withholding information from Tom? Would she have still withheld this know-how? Well, yes, she could have, but it would not have been in her own best interest. If her employer had a leadership value defined along the lines of constructive collaboration (as detailed in chapter 8), she would have run the risk of receiving the

FIGURE 10-1
Comparison of Karen's Old and New Rule Books

OLD *INSIDER'S RULE BOOK*	NEW *INSIDER'S RULE BOOK*
• Withholding information pays off.	• Collaboration pays off.
• Performance is judged on subjective criteria.	• Performance is judged on achieving specific and measurable goals.
• You look good when someone else looks bad.	• You look good when you look good. Making someone else look bad might reduce your leadership appraisal results.
• Personalities count more than performance.	• Performance counts for more than personalities.

Karen's Story (continued)

lowest rating (L5) of does not meet expectations. In the example we used in chapter 8, the lowest rating in this category was applicable to those who are characterized by their colleagues as hesitating to share information and resources. If her employer used these evaluations to determine Karen's merit increases, bonuses, and promotional opportunities (as explained in chapter 9), then clearly she would have sacrificed material gains. But if Tom were evaluated in the same manner, Karen would have had another reason to share her knowledge with Tom.

Let's take a look at this scenario from Tom's perspective. He, too, would have had goal sheets defining what he needed to accomplish. The most obvious benefit is that Tom would have had an objective standard for his performance that was shielded from personal attacks. But other, more subtle benefits would have accrued to him also.

Step 4 of the goal sheet asks about important links to other departments, areas, or people. It's very likely that Karen, or someone equally as knowledgeable about the financial systems, would have been identified as an important link on one of his goals. Tom's manager, or even his manager's boss, would have supplied this information because he would have had to review and discuss Tom's goal sheets.

If Karen had refused to share her knowledge, this issue would have been raised in Tom's performance update with his boss. He would clearly see that Tom was not getting the "education" he needed to succeed, and Tom's boss would have intervened.

Let's go one step further. Tom's manager very likely would have had a goal sheet relating to the training and development of his new employee, Tom. Furthermore, the training and development of subordinates would appear in the company's leadership appraisal form. If Tom's manager had any ambition to be promoted, he would take Tom's training seriously. In any case, Tom wouldn't have had to bear this burden on his own; his boss would have had incentive to support him.

That's all interesting speculation, albeit grounded in experience. But what did Karen have to say about it?

"I can't believe what you guys did," she announced after we walked her through the mechanics of a nonpolitical workplace. "I know you think I'm an idiot for doing what I did, but you've got to understand I just couldn't afford to lose my job.

"I think if it had been as clear as what you've laid out, then no, no, I don't think I would have felt so threatened. I mean, I know I could have done a good job and hit my goals, and that would have made me feel like I was doing something important. And I do think I would have been more likely to help teach Tom how things worked; I mean, I would have come off looking pretty good then, right?

"I guess it goes back to trust, you know, trust that your company is going to do the right thing, like not fire you just because you had a baby.

"So yeah, if you're asking me, it would have made a difference with me personally. But I've got to tell you, there are some people out there who just get it in their minds that they hate somebody—I mean really hate them. I've seen it before. I don't know what you can ever do about *that*." (Italics added.)

Among other things, no management system can change a hateful heart. But it can give that person the right incentives and let her know that however hateful she might feel, it's in her best interest not to act on it. Termination, a last resort that can send a powerful message, is always an option. As Jack Welch, CEO of General Electric, once remarked, "Sometimes it's easier to change people than to change people."[1]

Steve's Story

CASE STUDY: An aggressive marketing manager wants to improve his odds of being promoted.

POLITICAL RESPONSE: He reduces the number of perceived competitors for promotion.

First, Steve was absolutely right when he observed that getting promoted in his company was all about elimination, not selection. He had little motivation to excel and more motivation to make his colleague, Mike, look bad. Second, a strike against Mike was his bad first meeting with the company president, from which he could not recover. Because performance was all about personalities, Mike lost big time on the score. Lacking any objective criteria to judge his performance, it became a case of "one strike and you're out." It was all fairly predictable given the *Insider's Rule Book*.

What about this scenario would have changed in a nonpolitical workplace that employed the type of management system described in this book? Let's first take a quick look at how the rules have changed (see figure 10-2).

To begin with, in a nonpolitical workplace, all the product manag-

FIGURE 10-2
Comparison of Steve's Old and New Rule Books

OLD *INSIDER'S RULE BOOK*	NEW *INSIDER'S RULE BOOK*
• Promotion is a process of elimination, not selection.	• Promotion is a process of selection, not elimination. It is based on demonstrating proficiency in key leadership attribute areas.
• People don't have clear definable goals, other than to "keep the boss happy."	• Everyone has clearly defined goals, and rewards are linked to achieving them.
• You look good when someone else looks bad.	• You look good when you look good. Making someone else look bad might reduce your leadership appraisal results.
• Don't upset the higher-ups.	• Achieve your goals.

ers would have had specific goals that were directly tied to their rewards. These goals would also have directly supported their product line goals and ultimately the company's goals. Achievement, specific and measurable, would have replaced gut feelings as a basis for promotions. Of course, a senior executive could have still said he didn't like a worker, for whatever reason, but he'd have to explain why his dislike meant more than the individual's measurable performance. I've seen this maneuver numerous times before, and executives catch on quickly that with the new rules they simply don't come off well by placing personalities above performance.

In this new environment, Steve would have had little reason to sabotage Mike or anyone else for that matter. Since Steve's performance would be assessed on its own and not on a comparative basis, his best interest would have been served by focusing on achieving his own goals. Beyond that, if trust and integrity were a stated company value and measured by a 360-degree survey, Steve would have had additional incentive to do the right thing. While perhaps nobody would have known about his deleting Mike's hard drive, that type of destructive behavior is exhibited in many different ways and is often transparent to others.

What about Mike? Assessing his performance also would have been based on achieving his goals as defined in his goal sheet. If Steve had still deleted his hard dive, causing Mike to appear ill prepared in front of the new president, it would not have been a career breaker for Mike. Would it have still been embarrassing and regrettable? Yes. Would it have been the reason why he was passed over for a promotion? No. That's the difference.

So in a nonpolitical workplace, Steve would not have had the incentive to sabotage Mike. Even if he had tried, Steve's actions would not have even remotely had the same impact on Mike's career.

Once again, this account might sound like interesting speculation. Steve's reaction follows.

"Look, I wouldn't want to be a product manager for a company like the one you've described. One of my friends from graduate school works for a company just like that. They do everything you say to do,

Steve's Story (continued)

almost anyway. He thinks it's great, but I couldn't think of anything worse. I mean, come on! Goal sheets, peer evaluations? I'd feel—I don't know—handcuffed, I guess. No, it's definitely not a company I would ever go to work for."

Why say more?

Frank's Story

CASE STUDY: A plant manager gets angry when a young executive from headquarters uncovers productivity problems.

POLITICAL RESPONSE: The manager works to get him fired.

In perhaps one of the more cruelly ironic twists we've seen, the engineer in this case, Tony, demonstrated just the type of leadership the stockholders like to see—identifying an issue, raising awareness of it, and working to correct it using other people's experience with similar challenges. Yet it was in part because the plant manager cited a "lack of leadership" that the company fired the engineer.

What about the company and its *Insider's Rule Book* permitted this situation to happen? To begin with, the company operated under the rule of man—in this case, Frank's—and not the rule of law. Power and position dictated who was right instead of objective standards. This situation was especially true when it came to the more isolated parts of the company, like the stand-alone plant in Kentucky.

Second, the company had established few true performance measures that Tony could report on or for which goals, such as various productivity measures, were established. In addition, the company had no goal alignment, so while Tony thought the obvious goal was to improve productivity, Frank had a different agenda.

Certainly problems arose because the company neither defined what it meant by leadership (the specific, desired behavior and traits) nor devised measures for inspiring confidence (assuming that notion had ever been defined). Thus, the company increased the possibility of a man like Frank abusing his position as the sole evaluator of Tony's abilities.

How could a nonpolitical workplace, governed by the type of management system described in this book, have helped? To answer that, let's quickly compare the old *Insider's Rule Book* with the new one (see figure 10-3).

How would things have been different if the company had just used goal sheets to ensure goal alignment? Imagine if, upon arriving

Frank's Story (continued)

for his assignment, Tony and Frank had worked together to develop Tony's goals. Assume, too, that Bill, Frank's boss, had reviewed their goal sheets. All three men would have certainly had a better understanding of why Tony was there and what he was supposed to do.

Going a step further, if the company had created a role profile for Tony's new position, it would have been clear from the start what Tony should be doing while at the Little Beaverton plant. Likewise, if the company as a whole had defined its vision and values and had gone through all the exercises to create a road map (including defining goals and initiatives to achieve them) then the plant would have been integrated with the rest of the organization. The organization's expectations for the plant and its contribution would have been clearly defined. At that point, Frank would have probably welcomed all the help he could get.

What did Frank have to say about all these proposed changes? Well, he had an interesting point of view, which, from what we've seen, is consistent with his personal philosophy.

"You're on to something, I'll give you that. At one point in my

FIGURE 10-3
Comparison of Frank's Old and New Rule Books

OLD *INSIDER'S RULE BOOK*	NEW *INSIDER'S RULE BOOK*
• Might makes right. Power and position dictate who's right.	• Objective standards and reasoned judgment determine what's right, which is the only question (not *who's* right).
• Leadership is a vaguely defined, subjective term that can be an effective weapon when used as such.	• Leadership is broken down into specific, measurable traits and characteristics, and is measured by a 360-degree evaluation.
• Protect your turf and ensure your power.	• Collaboration is recognized and pays off. Power is granted to those who demonstrate they can successfully lead others and achieve results.
• Isolation allows you to consolidate your power. Outsiders are threats.	• Align goals. Your goals support someone else's, and you need to support the company's goals.

career I spent a couple of years in a bottling plant, and it was run pretty much like you described. Everyone knew what they had to do to contribute to the goals of the organization, and everyone's rewards were tied to it. Certain types of behavior were really encouraged, and everyone pretty much seemed to do the right thing. The results for the plant were pretty good—no, strike that—they were outstanding.

"But I wouldn't want to share power like that. Look, I'll be honest with you. What gives me the thrill isn't hitting some productivity number. That's too abstract for me. Yeah, I know, one for all and all for one and all that, but it just doesn't do it for me. You wanna know what does? Walking down any hallway in this plant and knowing I can do whatever I want, whenever I want. The fact that everybody here knows it makes it even better. They're all afraid of me, and I know you don't like that, but when I say, 'Stand on your head,' you'd better believe they do it.

"If our company did everything you recommend, all that would go away. I'd be forced to work with other people, I couldn't control anything the way I do now, I'd have to deliver results that weren't always set by me. I'd lose it all.

"But if it happened anyway, yeah, I'd have to go along with it. I'm less than five years away from retirement; I wouldn't want to blow it. It would just be a shame, that's all."

A shame? I'm not so sure every one of his employees would agree. Do you?

Brent's Story

CASE STUDY: A manager is afraid to make a recommendation that would save the company millions of dollars, because it reflects poorly on a previous decision made by the company's president.

POLITICAL RESPONSE: The manager buries the recommendation.

Brent's dilemma was simple: If he told the truth, that there was no justification for keeping the plant open, he could embarrass the president, who built it. He concluded, not so surprising, that he had to find a justification to keep the plant open. That justification turned out to be the Internet and the promise of explosive growth in handheld electronic games.

What about the company's *Insider's Rule Book* encouraged Brent's behavior and ultimately this misuse of funds? Let's go with the obvious things first. In Brent's company, addressing a problem wasn't so much a case of finding the right answer as much as figuring out how an approach would make people look. People's careers were known to have been sidetracked by presenting information that indicated a powerful person had once made a mistake (even if that information was being used for some unrelated purpose or that particular mistake had been made long ago).

People who study this type of behavior say that the Mafia maintains its power more from the perceived threat of violence than from actual violence. It only takes a couple of incidents—for example, people gone missing—for everyone else to fall in line. After a short while, rumors and innuendo perpetuate the growing reputation.

In Brent's company, the workers believe that indirectly making one of the higher-ups look bad can be career limiting. It doesn't really take much to build and perpetuate that perception and then to burn it into the *Insider's Rule Book*.

Who stands to gain and who stands to lose? was one of the first questions people in the company wanted to answer before working on any project. Brent, feeling as if he was in a no-win situation, built an entire justification around it. In the end, he suffered a loss from it, too.

Brent could have used this opportunity to sharpen his skills as an analyst by delving into alternatives, conducting rigorous economic analysis, and reaching valuable insight. Instead, he became what's commonly called a "flunky," someone who is all too quick to suspend his integrity and know-how to support a superior. Temporarily, this approach might secure his position in the company, but longer term, it erodes his value and skills in the marketplace. He won't even realize it, however, until he has to look for a new job.

How could a nonpolitical workplace, governed by the type of management system described in this book, have changed this situation? Let's quickly compare the old *Insider's Rule Book* with the new one (see figure 10-4).

In a nonpolitical workplace, management sets clear goals and ties people's rewards directly to them. In Brent's case, presumably one of the company's goals would have related to profitability. Assuming the rewards were material, the president would have had a sizable incentive to obtain the real economic analysis of the plant in question. Secure in this knowledge, Brent would have felt encouraged to tell the truth.

Yet in a broader sense, the culture of the company would be altered, especially if it had identified truth and integrity among its core values. If its leadership appraisals reflected this change, then the invisible cultural forces that influenced Brent would have instead guided him

FIGURE 10-4
Comparison of Brent's Old and New Rule Books

OLD *INSIDER'S RULE BOOK*	NEW *INSIDER'S RULE BOOK*
• Your job is to make your boss look good.	• Your job is to achieve your goals.
• Shoot the messenger.	• Those who tell the truth, even under difficult circumstances, will be rewarded and held out as role models.
• Analysis should be skewed based on how the outcome will make someone look or on the outcome someone wants to see.	• Analysis is driven by a pursuit of the truth.
• The root question of any analysis is Who stands to win, who stands to lose?	• The root question of any analysis is What's right for the company?

Brent's Story (continued)

to conduct a true, rigorous economic analysis that would provide the best alternative for the company.

How does Brent feel about this possibility? When we shared the inner workings of a nonpolitical workplace, here's what he said.

"We should have had this type of thing a long time ago," he began. "I think it could have changed a lot of things. The problem with it, though, is I just don't see the senior people freely giving up control. I mean, they have it pretty good right now. They get a good paycheck and an even better bonus, when not much ever changes. We make products, people buy them, we make money. Yeah, our earnings go up and down, so does our stock price, but so what? It doesn't change their compensation as much as you might think. So from where they sit, why give up all this power, especially after you clawed your way up to get it?

"Is your approach in the best interests of employees and shareholders? Yes, of course. Is it in the best interests of the few people with all the power? Ultimately, yes, but you're going to have a hard time convincing them. But I hope you do because, well, let's just say that this isn't the way I pictured myself. There should be more to work than covering your backside. If I had a choice I'd leave, but at this point I don't know where I'd go."

Tamara's Story

CASE STUDY: A marketing analyst is concerned that she's not quite up to leading a project, within her job description, that she's been assigned.

POLITICAL RESPONSE: She befriends the boss and compels him to make a less popular coworker accountable.

If there is an overarching theme to all these stories, Tamara's case epitomizes it. Once again, a political mastermind won something for herself, while the company lost. In this case, Tamara successfully lobbied her boss, Jeff; abdicated her responsibility; and shifted it neatly to her coworker, Susan. This dodge meant less work and effort and more unscheduled time for Tamara. In addition, it saved her from the potential embarrassment of being discovered in a lie, for she was incapable of doing a job she claimed she could do in her interview. The organization, however, lost a hard-working, intelligent, and highly effective employee as a direct result of Tamara's scheme. Yet again the company needs to consider the recruiting fees to replace Susan and all the associated costs of having a new employee come up to speed. Those costs are all obvious and calculable.

Another, perhaps more subtle cost to the organization harks back to its *Insider's Rule Book,* which is always open to changes. Any employee who had observed Tamara's machinations would have concluded, quite reasonably, that it was possible to shift his workload to a coworker by befriending his boss and lobbying for it behind the scenes. While surely not every manager could be manipulated as Jeff was, nothing structurally in the company's management system would prevent it from happening. People might wonder, *Why not try it? Heck, it's worth a shot.*

As a consequence, this type of manipulative behavior grows. Maybe it's not repeated in exactly the same way, but the underlying message—anything is possible if one can get on the good side of the boss—spreads and results in equally destructive behavior. Cynicism builds, and good people circulate their résumés to other companies. It doesn't happen

Tamara's Story (continued)

overnight, but it does happen. And when it does, it's difficult to reverse. That's the real cost.

What about the management of Children in Need permitted Tamara to succeed in shifting her official responsibilities to an unsuspecting coworker? To begin with, her boss was accountable only to himself and not to the organization. He was free to use and abuse the people who reported to him in any way that he saw fit.

Neither Tamara nor Susan—nor Jeff, for that matter—was truly an integral part of Children in Need. In a superficial sense, someone could read their job descriptions and take a guess at how they fit into the larger organization, but their work and their goals remained largely autonomous. Consequently, their duties and responsibilities could be manipulated at will.

Furthermore, while the official policy manuals would never have condoned what Jeff did, there really wasn't anything preventing him from changing job descriptions and duties for his direct reports. In some respects, what happened occurred simply because it could. Imagine, for example, how people would drive without any posted speed limits or fines. Would people speed? Of course. Why? Because they could.

In the most basic sense, the organization's laissez-faire style of leadership gave rise to abuse that simply went unchecked. Regrettably, this situation is not uncommon.

So what would have changed under a nonpolitical workplace? To begin with, let's review a comparison of the old *Insider's Rule Book* with the new one (see figure 10-5).

In a nonpolitical workplace Jeff would have been required to complete role profiles and to develop goal sheets for both Tamara's and Susan's positions. These documents would have been a matter of official record and would have been reviewed by both his boss as well as human resources. Thus, the women's roles would have been largely immutable. Furthermore, Jeff would have developed a proper balance between these two positions because (a) they would have been drafted even before Jeff interviewed Tamara, and (b) Jeff would have known that he would have to live with these job descriptions for some time so he'd work to ensure they were "right."

Second, even if Jeff had succumbed to Tamara's manipulations, he would not have been able to operate alone. To change Susan's role, Tom would have been required to make official amendments to her role profile and goal sheets, which would have needed approval from his boss. Presumably Jeff's boss would have been more objective, and if he wasn't, then HR officials (who facilitate the process) would have raised questions.

Yet the dynamics also might have changed Susan's behavior as well. Given clear, unambiguous personal responsibilities and goals, and rewards that were strictly tied to them, Susan might have finally felt comfortable pushing back. After all, with a clear understanding of her roles, goals, and rewards, she could have posed the obvious question, "How does this new role of project leader fit in with my duties, Jeff?"

Refusing to cooperate would not have jeopardized her rewards, because they would have already been tied to a set of objective goals. Second, her performance evaluation would have been influenced not

FIGURE 10-5
Comparison of Tamara's Old and New Rule Books

OLD *INSIDER'S RULE BOOK*

- Befriending your boss is more important than doing a good job.

- People who "are not in the circle" are vulnerable, and you can easily be take advantage of them.

- Your official job description, and those of your colleagues, means little. It's whatever your boss desires at the moment.

- Your goals never really have to be committed to; you can get them changed or even eliminated if you're in your boss's good graces.

NEW *INSIDER'S RULE BOOK*

- Achieving your official goals, and demonstrating the company's values, is the most important thing you can do.

- Principals come before personalities.

- Your role profile and goal sheets can be altered only by mutual agreement with your manager, her boss, and Human Resources.

- Your rewards are driven by achieving your goals, which can't be changed without due process.

Tamara's Story (continued)

just by Jeff, who might have held a grudge if she wouldn't play along, but by a 360-degree survey of her peers.

Furthermore, Susan could hardly have been accused of not being a team player, because in fact she was regarded as being highly committed to achieving her goals and doing the best job possible. And if Jeff was not willing to change her role profile or goal sheet officially, then how important could his request be?

Finally, Jeff's role as a manager would have been evaluated by his boss, who would check Jeff's ability to train, develop, and motivate his employees. This system would have given Jeff incentive to work with Tamara to build her capabilities to run the project and to treat Susan fairly. Clearly, attempting to circumvent the management system to shift more responsibility to Susan would have put him in jeopardy.

In brief, the management system of a nonpolitical workplace would have made Tamara's attempts to fob off her responsibilities quite transparent. Equally important, Jeff's willingness to go along with them would have also been transparent, and he would have risked his own career.

Would Tamara change her behavior in a nonpolitical workplace? I'll let her tell you.

"You know, I'm kind of surprised more companies don't do more stuff like this," Tamara told us. "I mean, it sounds like a lot of common sense, right? Just Management 101. But the thing is, no matter how simple it looks, or how straightforward, people don't want to give up what they've got.

"Look, once you figure out how it really works inside a company, or a not-for-profit like Children in Need, you realize how much it beats working for a living. I'm kidding, of course, but there's some truth to it. I mean, the system you've set up requires that everyone hits their goals to get rewarded. I get rewarded now anyway, and I can normally make things go in my favor. I know how to work the system. So why would I want to change that?

"So no, I wouldn't want to see it done here. But if the question is, What would I have done differently if Children in Need had a system like that in place when I joined them? I don't know, maybe nothing. But I know Jeff, and there's no way he would have gone along with me in that case. He cares too much about his career, and the way you've set things up, he really would have been putting a lot at risk just to make me happy. He likes me, but not that much. So would it have made a difference, yeah, I guess it would have in the end."

Reviewing all the comments made by the five people we profiled, they are consistent in two respects. First, a nonpolitical workplace would have affected their behavior. And second, for the most part, they'd prefer not to work in a nonpolitical workplace. Are these the kind of people who will make your organization prosper? Since these people are exactly the type you *wouldn't* want working in your organization, however, can you think of a better endorsement for implementing a nonpolitical workplace?

Notes

1   Jack Welch, CEO of General Electric, in a conversation with the author, 1999.

CHAPTER 11

Can't Delay Satisfaction?
Eight Quick Tips and Handy Tricks

It is never too late to be what you might have been.
—GEORGE ELIOT

I think it's obvious at this point that the structural changes we're recommending to reform a political workplace won't happen overnight. Yet the only way to mitigate the enemy within successfully is to change the *Insider's Rule Book*. The question then is, What, if anything, can be done in the meantime? Are there any "quick tips" we can implement in short order that will at least move the work culture in the right direction?

The answer is yes, but proceed with caution. There's a risk that by implementing a couple of innovative ideas and experiencing a few early wins, an organization will grow complacent. *Heck, that wasn't so hard,* the manager thinks. *We're making progress. Do we really need to make changes to our management systems, too?*

Take the following top eight ideas for what they are, simple ideas that can be implemented relatively quickly to produce some progress. Although hardly an exhaustive list, it should give you something to think about and help you generate some ideas of your own. Bear in mind, however, that these innovative ideas yield greater benefits when you institute the components of a nonpolitical workplace.

Have Nonfinancial Employees Present the Monthly Performance Results to the Organization

This idea is what economists like to refer to as "an elegant solution." It is a simple concept, is easy to implement, and yields powerful results. Here's how it works.

In most companies, accounting closes the books at the end of the month and then issues the financial results (most commonly in some form of an income statement). In large and mid-size companies, a finance person (or department) reviews the results and compares them to the plan, or the budget. That person determines whether the company is doing better or worse than the plan called for in specific areas. The more significant question, however, is, *Why* are we doing better or worse? In the parlance of finance professionals, this process is called conducting *variance analysis*. When this analysis is complete, the financial results are amended with commentary, neatly packaged, and distributed to the organization. The intent, a noble one to be sure, is to communicate to everyone how the company is doing.

But here's the catch. For most employees, receiving this monthly report is akin to getting a summary of U.K. cricket scores. It might be interesting, perhaps, but it's easily ignored. Likewise, most employees find the financial results are wholly disconnected, at least so it seems, from what they do every day.

This view represents a big missed opportunity. Remember that when people feel like they don't know what's going on, it's difficult for them to feel part of something larger than themselves—that is, the company. Reviews of the organization's financial and operational performance compared to plan don't have to be dry. The numbers don't merely reflect what people—or employees, competitors, suppliers, alliance partners, and so on—have done. The numbers actually reflect a story, and it's the ability both to communicate and to comprehend that story that bonds workers together. It weaves their own daily efforts into the fabric of what's happening in the company.

So what can we do about it? Change the rules, and give people incentive to communicate and understand the story. Specifically, have nonfinancial employees present the company's results to the organization or, if it's a large company, to their division or business unit. That way, engineers, marketing and human resource professionals, and so on will each take a turn at presenting the results.

Anyone giving the update will need to take the time to understand the results, as well as how those results are presented, and craft a presentation to explain them to their coworkers. Not only will the presenters gain an appreciation for what happened during the period under review, but they'll gain valuable knowledge about how the company works, especially beyond their own area, and how it measures its performance. In other words, they'll build their business literacy. After this experience, they'll understand those cricket scores and what those scores mean for them. This newfound appreciation will also make it much more likely that they'll pay attention to their colleagues' future business reviews.

The most common objection I hear to this idea is that "it will take people away from their work." That's the whole point. It's insularity that builds up barriers between departments and people. When people understand and appreciate what's happening in the company as a whole—not just from passively listening to the CFO recount results but from gaining firsthand knowledge from personally digging into it—it makes all the difference.

Likewise, I often hear people object, "Come on, isn't that finance's job to report the results?" Traditionally, yes, and that's what makes this new approach innovative. Beyond that, restricting the ownership of understanding and reporting the company's results to just one group—be it finance or any other—gives the wrong impression that the information is not everyone's concern, but rather *it's a finance thing.* That's like being on a football team where only the quarterback and wide receivers keep track of the score. Ridiculous, right? Everyone on the team wants to know if they're winning or losing the game. In fact, isn't that a surefire way you can recognize a team *as* a team?

Start breaking down those departmental barriers by letting everyone understand if and, more important, why the company is winning the game. For some individuals, just knowing that their turn to present the monthly performance results is coming is enough to prompt them to learn the business and how all the various aspects of it come together. For others, especially those without formal business training or those who might be relatively isolated in their work, something more formal might be required.

Teach Everyone How the Business Works

How does the business work? Every manager—and, I would argue, every employee—should be able to answer this question and know well. It will help people make better decisions and build organization-wide cooperation and a collective sense of team.

Professional sports organizations are the common models for describing a team because every player knows the rules, the role of each position and how it contributes to the organization's success, and, of course, how the individual players fit in. In football, for example, a defensive end recognizes a good wide receiver when he sees one, even though the former works on defense and the latter works on offense. They know what everyone else is supposed to be doing and how all the individual roles contribute to winning. Sounds pretty simple, doesn't it? So why don't we see the same widespread clarity in most organizations? What about the institutional dynamics or *Insider's Rule Book* explains it?

In many companies, only a handful of people really know how the business works, or how all the different pieces of the puzzle fit together, and that's chiefly because it hasn't been explained to anyone else. The *Insider's Rule Book* says, "Keep your head down and keep your boss happy." It doesn't say anything about learning how your organization works as a company. So the marketing people live in a world of sales, operations people live in a world of manufacturing, HR people live in a world of employee recruitment and turnover, and accounting people live in a world of the month-end close. Sound familiar? It's as if the defensive end barely knows that a wide receiver is supposed to catch the ball and run.

What do we mean exactly by this term *how the company works*? Some people use the term *business model* as a shorthand way of saying the same thing; it's *a conceptual understanding of what the business is all about.* An illustration of a business model follows. You'll see how even just a few short paragraphs can capture what makes a business tick.

At one of the world's largest publishing and direct-mail businesses, "new names," or those people who have never bought from the company before, are brought into the company's database when they subscribe to the flagship magazine (which has a circulation counted in the *millions* of copies sold). This database is known as the company's "front door." The question then is, How to capitalize on these new names?

Apart from publishing a well-known magazine, the company also develops books, videotapes, CDs, and general merchandise catalogs that are targeted to appeal to the magazine's average reader. When a new subscriber's name enters the database, it triggers the mailing of a direct-mail piece that should appeal to that reader. If the reader accepts that offer, then another one follows a couple of weeks later. In fact, an entire stream of offerings follow, which is why this process is known as "streaming a new name."

If the reader rejects the first offer or any that follow, then that information is added to the database as well. But don't worry, the company isn't about to give up yet. From its intensive research and knowledge accumulated over many years, its people know just the alternative offer to send to you (and what to do when you finally accept one of them).

The fantastic part about this business is that it can be hugely profitable because there's no middleman. The publisher sells directly to you, the final buyer, and keeps the middleman's mark-up. In addition, the publisher builds up a personal relationship with you and learns invaluable knowledge about your buying habits.

So what's really necessary to make this process work well? To begin with, the manager needs great editors who know what the "average" reader wants. Then he wants insightful database managers to comb through the purchasing data and find important buying patterns—for example, which people bought the *Classics from the Old West* CD *and* the book *Tales of Gunslingers and Outlaws*. Next, he needs a creative staff to develop fresh approaches to direct-mail presentations. He also requires both an operations team, which can produce everything effectively but inexpensively, and a purchasing team that helps secure raw materials at a competitive price.

I could go on, but you have a good sense of this company's business model. How could we get everyone in the company to understand it and appreciate how all the separate parts contribute to the organization's over-all success? How can we start to take down the artificial barriers that have built up over the years?

We could take either a formal approach or an informal one. In a formal approach, we could create a classroom-like curriculum, something like "Our Business 101," to teach all of the managers the business model. Personally, I prefer a more informal approach.

A brown-bag-lunch series can be highly effective and is less intimidat-ing than a formal classroom setting. Once a month during lunch, for example, a manager from one of the functional areas or departments could present what his people do and how they do it. He could also ex-plain how he measures their performance, with what other areas they work most closely, and how they contribute to the company's overall suc-cess. As an incentive to go to these events, people could earn points for attendance that could then be redeemed for gift certificates or other in-ducements.

Another informal approach is for a company to take advantage of its own internal web site and create a presentation or demonstration of how the entire business model works. Companies get really creative in this area. I've seen everything from simple PowerPoint slides describing the model to cartoon animation using images to convey key aspects of the model (like a new name entering a consumer database). One company I know of created a board game that simulated the business. Groups of forty people or more were trained in sessions by breaking into smaller groups of five or six, playing the game, and discussing the results after-ward.

What's important in communicating the company's business model to the organization is that people learn to understand and appreciate what everyone else does to contribute to the organization's success. That's a great first step in tearing down walls and building a collective sense of being part of a team.

Open the Books

"Opening up the books" simply means letting everyone know how the organization is doing. Many companies think just distributing the financial results with a little commentary is sufficient, but they need to go well beyond that if they want to unite the organization as a single team. As we discussed in the first two ideas, if people don't know how to read or interpret the results, the reports aren't useful.

Beyond that, companies do not live by financial statistics alone. In fact, as authors Kaplan and Norton have illustrated in their groundbreaking work on balanced scorecards, financial results only provide a good look in the company's rearview mirror.[1] Companies also need to share their leading indicators of future performance, which are usually operational statistics.

In chapter 8 we discussed the need to identify what drives success in the business and the company's critical processes and to devise appropriate measures. These are the sort of leading indicators that any organization should have. Assuming a company has identified these measures, it should monitor them just as closely as the financial measures and communicate them in the same fashion. Once again, it will be important that managers are trained to understand what all the numbers mean. Too few companies actually do share this information, but those that do report an enormous increase in the breadth and depth of their people's understanding of the business, which, in turn, fosters increased cooperation and team spirit.

My recommendation is to open up the books one step further. The company might be communicating its key measures (financial and nonfinancial), but what about its goals and progress toward those goals? This information is what gives people a true sense of what the score is and whether they are winning the game.

Technology can be a big help here with capturing and reporting data through enterprise application systems (EAS), creating electronic "dashboards" for key measures, leveraging the Internet and company portals for one-stop shopping for information, and providing endless other possibilities. Of course, it's easy to get carried away and become so involved in building systems that they never actually get implemented, but by sticking to the basics, technology can provide considerable assistance in keeping people informed and feeling a part of the team.

Of course, there is no substitute for face-to-face meetings for people are still a pretty social bunch. (After all, we counted on each other for survival for millions of years, give or take.) The two tools I recommend are the *weekly huddle* and a *monthly business exchange.*

The weekly huddle is a *department meeting to discuss how the department is doing against its goals.* The huddle usually involves going around the table and asking each manager for an update. Are we on still on track to meet our next important milestones? Have we encountered any surprises? How have they been dealt with? What more can we do? Does it look like we will achieve our goals?

While the format will be much the same department to department, the discussions will be markedly different. Marketing might talk about specific marketing campaigns that are scheduled, operations might discuss productivity improvement efforts, accounting might consider its efforts to shave two days off the close, and human resources might examine its initiative to increase the retention rate by 5 percent. The point is that every week each department should set aside time to huddle together and review its progress toward its goals.

While the weekly huddle's focus is on departmental goals, the purpose of the monthly business exchange is *to report on the company's progress.* To prepare for this meeting, senior managers will need to meet with each of their department heads for an update on the progress that they've each made toward their goals. In this way, each functional leader can provide the organization with highlights of all the progress made in his or her area during the month.

In these meetings, the CEO should also report on the overall performance of the organization. Of course, this account involves a review of the company's financials, but it is also a time to report on other key measures. Depending on what critical event happened during the month or on what milestones might be coming up that month, the focus of these sessions will change.

Communication is a two-way street. Although I feel the purpose of the monthly exchange is to let each manager—or every employee, depending on the organization's size—know how the enterprise is doing, it's also a time when people can ask their leaders questions.

This type of session signals an open communication style that no official proclamation can match. It also instills a sense of a collective team effort, and it reinforces the concept of winning as an organization when each department makes an important contribution.

Design a Formal Conflict Resolution Process

Here's a true story. While the specifics of this case might be different from what you've experienced personally, you've undoubtedly encountered a similar situation.

One of the largest American Indian nations in the United States was organized by business units, two of which were so large that they commanded their own independent human resource departments. One of those HR departments also acted on behalf of all of the smaller business units. For a long time, this arrangement worked well, but after experiencing explosive growth in revenues and employees, conflicts arose. Employees got confused as to what the "official" policy was on everything from sick pay (one business unit's policy was four paid sick days a year, while the other allowed only two) to when overtime pay kicked in (thirty-five hours in one business unit, forty hours in the other).

The solution seemed simple enough. The two separate HR departments just needed to agree on an overall policy. Surely they could do that. Although everyone agreed with the concept, it just never happened. Meetings got canceled as emergencies arose, and when the parties did meet, there was a great deal of generalized talk but no concrete agreements. This situation went on for more than two years.

It sounds incredible, until you reflect on your own experience. Everyone who's been in the work world for a while has a story of how a conflict between two factions in the same organization failed to reach a timely resolution. Sometimes those conflicts arise in a single department and still go unresolved. So what can a company do?

Every organization can use a formal conflict resolution process. It's pretty straightforward. Conflicts are discussed in a formal process (described below). If the parties fail to reach an agreement, they take their case to the next level. If need be, it can go right up to the CEO, but it rarely does as it would reflect unfavorably on the senior managers who could not resolve their own disputes. Here's how the process works.

Let's say two product managers from separate product lines each want to launch their new products in the same quarter of the year, and each believes that the other's product launch will diminish his results (or steal his thunder). The two parties come to an impasse. At this point the formal process is triggered.

They schedule a meeting to discuss the issue with each product manager's boss. The meeting should be held within two weeks, even if that means meeting at seven o'clock in the morning or seven o'clock at night to accommodate everybody's schedule. In turn, each manager would inform her boss (perhaps they share the same one) with a one-sentence description of the conflict and the date when it will be discussed. The managers want to alert their bosses for two reasons. If the managers cannot resolve the issue, it will be coming their way, and it puts healthy pressure on the participants to reach an agreeable conclusion (or at the very least show up) at the meeting. In our example, let's assume that the two product managers report to two separate product line managers. These four people then participate in the meeting, and the senior vice president of marketing (to whom both of the product line managers report) receives notice of the meeting and the nature of the conflict.

At the meeting, one product manager has ten minutes to present his perspective, after which the other product manager is expected to paraphrase what he heard to ensure he understood it. Then the order is reversed. Afterward, the group brainstorms alternatives and agrees on one that would successfully resolve the conflict. If they cannot agree, the case goes to the next level.

In this example, the senior vice president of marketing would make the deciding call, because both product line managers report to her. She would be the last stop in this case. If a conflict arose within the ranks of operations, then the senior vice president of operations would most likely be the last stop. If a conflict arose in the lower ranks between two different departments, then the managers from both sides would try to find a resolution. If it escalated up the line, eventually the senior vice presidents of marketing and operations would address it. Only if they could not resolve the dispute would it go as far as the CEO.

This process formalizes and discloses conflicts that can hamstring an organization. In addition, it greatly accelerates the conflict resolution process, which can otherwise be quite time- and energy-consuming. The traditional lobbying and working the corridors to win support for a position eat up quite a bit of time, time that has become a scarce resource in today's hypercompetitive markets.

This formalized process works in the companies that have implemented it because the process is clear and out in the open. Everyone therefore knows how it should be handled. Also, there is no stigma associated with calling a meeting to resolve an issue when that's the accepted official process. (In some company cultures, people prefer to avoid looking like they're overreacting, even if it means a conflict goes unresolved for months.) Finally, using the formal, aboveboard resolution process also helps to depoliticize conflicts.

Use the Camcorder Image

How many decisions would be made differently if the players knew the world was watching? Here's one example. A jury awarded plaintiffs more than $4 billion in a case against one of the Big Three automakers. Why? What had enraged the jury to the point that it would call for a multibillion-dollar award?

The jury heard testimony about an internal memo that computed the company's cost at $200,000 for each auto fatality and about two dollars for each car sold with the gas tank placed where it could explode on impact. The memo said the cost of moving the tank was about eight dollars. Based on this calculation—the calculation of what a life was worth, in essence—the company opted not to move the tank. The jury found this decision outrageous and delivered a high punitive damage award.

Do you think the company would have made a different decision had it known one day the world would find out about it? Of course, it would have. Its problems look quite different in public, with everyone watching. The managers knew right from wrong. It's just that in private they succumbed to the temptation and thought they could get away with their decision. Let's see, should they spend two dollars per car and risk a life lost to an exploding car or spend eight dollars each to move the tank? Hmmm.

Doing the right thing in business is always easier when you know that the rationale for making your decision will be made public. To keep yourself honest, imagine a camcorder recording all of your decisions. Should you terminate an employee or promote one? Should you join forces with another product group to come up with a synergistic campaign or not? You get the picture.

While I don't know of any company that actually uses a camcorder, some companies bring decision making out into the open by communicating decisions and sharing the rationale for them with broad groups within the company. One company, for example, pairs up executives from various departments and has them explain any employee termination they've made in the last quarter and the rationale for it. It's a way of adding some checks and balances and ensuring that no department becomes too isolated.

Other companies run "spot audits" not just for accounting and finance, but also for HR issues as well. They publish their HR policies and guidelines, which they expect everyone to observe, but much like any accounting policy, nothing absolutely prevents them from being neglected or even abused. Spot audits, and even the possibility of a spot audit, can give someone pause before ignoring a policy. Furthermore, they send a message that the company cares about its HR policies as much as it does its accounting polices. In other words, the company values its people as much as it values its money.

Host an Annual Awards Show

"What type of employee do we really want working here?" Every company needs to answer that question. Once it has, then it needs to figure out how to attract those people.

Changing bonus structures and other forms of compensation can take (a great deal of) time. Just getting everybody (or nearly everybody) to agree to such changes presents a significant challenge. In the meantime, if you want to do something more immediate to broadcast who you want working in your organization, organize an awards show.

In chapter 7, I mentioned the annual employee awards ceremony American Express holds. It is fabulous, what with guest speakers like Bill Cosby and all, but it's a tad expensive for most companies. A company doesn't have to go that far to demonstrate whom it wants its employees to model themselves after.

It helps a great deal if a company has already defined the leadership characteristics and behaviors the employee needs to succeed and has linked them to personal rewards (all discussed in chapter 7). But these issues are not absolute prerequisites. A company can still develop an annual awards program. All it needs is a nominating committee to determine the classifications for the awards (again, made easier if the leadership characteristics have been defined), how the final winners will be decided, and finally the agenda and location of the ceremonies.

One telecommunications company decided to run an annual awards program and pulled together a team of six people, representing various functions and levels within the organization, to produce it. They came up with various awards for the people who sparked the greatest innovation that year, most represented the company's values, demonstrated the greatest commitment to employee development, spearheaded the greatest productivity gain, and so on.

This awards team decided that all employees could nominate anyone else in the company, but they would have to offer a clear, written explanation as to why their nominee should be considered. The team also convened groups of experts for each award to evaluate the nominees, to determine the finalists, and to choose the winners. The team flew the finalists to the awards ceremony (the first was held in New Orleans) and gave the winners titanium plaques commemorating the event. The team decided against cash awards because it thought they would in some way negate the awards' higher purpose. A Dixieland jazz band was hired for the ceremony's entertainment, and the event was a resounding success, being credited with helping to reduce turnover by 20 percent.

Other companies have simply combined the annual awards with their holiday parties or company picnics, and others hold quarterly awards in the company cafeteria. Whatever your budget and your organization's needs, your intent should be to reward the behaviors you want others in the organization to emulate.

Build Your Competitor's Business Plan

One of the most interesting exercises your company can undertake is to build your competitor's business plan. Most of you are accustomed to developing business plans for your own companies, but building one for your competitor is an eye-opening experience.

While this illustration is for a company, the process can be applied at a lower level for a division, a product line, or even individual products. Here's how it works. You begin by pulling together a team of four to six people who preferably represent the company's various major functions. Second, have the team identify your major competitor. While you can certainly include other competitors as well, it's best to "get the feel" for the exercise first by focusing on your chief rival.

In the third step, the team studies your competitor in detail. The team has numerous options for information gathering. They can:

- Talk to people who worked for the rival prior to joining your company and probe their knowledge.

- Visit the Internet chat rooms where your rival is discussed (while you're at it, check out your own too) to see what people are saying.

- Ask the Wall Street analysts who cover your stock for their coverage of your competitor and for any off-the-record information they've heard.

- Contact the major associations for your industry for their impressions.

- Ask your suppliers, if they do business with your competitor, for their perspectives.

- Gather all of the available public information—annual reports, press releases, earnings announcements, and so on.

Next, get the team members to place themselves in your rival's shoes and ask them to complete a SWOT (strengths, weaknesses, opportunities, threats) analysis of the rival. They should identify the company's major segments, customers, and suppliers. Where is the company most vulnerable, and what should its people be doing that they're not doing now? Where are their biggest opportunities, and what should they be doing about them?

The team actually builds a mock business plan for your rival in the fifth step. This model should include a *marketing plan* that details the marketing opportunities and the initiatives that should be undertaken to achieve them; an *operational plan* that outlines programs to reduce costs, improve efficiency and delivery, and so on; a *capital plan* that outlines any major capital programs, such as a new plant and IT systems; and finally, a projected *financial statement,* which reflects the direction of all the other plans.

In step 6, the team presents its model to senior management and answers any questions. If the team has prepared a good plan, management will have many questions. Trust me. The seventh and final step is to share their key findings with the rest of the organization and to incorporate the knowledge into your own company's plans.

If this project sounds like a fair amount of work, it is. But you can present the idea and get it approved quickly, and the team can get up and running within a week. The benefits of this exercise will begin to accrue immediately to the work team as the members learn how to gather and interpret competitive information. The benefits to the company are two-fold. The obvious benefit includes a penetrating understanding of your chief competitor(s), which, in turn, will serve to sharpen your own plans and position. The subtle benefit is the message to the employees: Our competition has been identified, and it's out there, not in here. People tend to be motivated by competition, and the more clearly you can direct their energy and enthusiasm to your competitors, the better off you'll be.

Prescreen Job Applicants for Desired Behavior

Your company probably screens its applicants now, but there might be an opportunity for some fine-tuning here.

If your company has defined its values and has developed a leadership appraisal form (like the type discussed in chapter 7), then I would recommend describing this process to applicants before they are hired. In chapter 10, when we revisited the five people whose political machinations were profiled in this book and asked them for their reactions to a nonpolitical workplace, they all had reservations about working in such an environment. That simply goes to show that you can identify and screen out individuals who are prone to political behavior before they have a chance to disrupt the organization. The commonsense advice here is to avoid hiring problem people in the first place. As the old expression goes, an ounce of prevention is worth a pound of cure.

Okay, what if your company has not yet defined its values and has not developed a leadership appraisal form and process? In that case, you can still ask telling questions of any applicant, such as:

- Tell me about a time when a conflict arose between you and someone else in your organization. How did you approach it? What was the outcome?

- What do you do when you simply don't get along with someone you work with?

- Here's the scenario. Your favorite cousin is having a problem with one of his coworkers over who's going to get the larger piece of a scarce resource. He is not the sharpest tool in the shed, but you love him and want to see him do well. What advice would you give him?

- Have you ever been forced into a situation where you felt you needed to take steps to protect your position, steps that under normal circumstances you wouldn't consider?

You might reword these questions or come up with some of your own. While I wouldn't ask one candidate all of these questions, they do illustrate that a job candidate's propensity for political behavior—as for creativity or commitment—can be determined.

Parting Thoughts

I mentioned at the start of this chapter that these innovative ideas should fire up your imagination about what you can do to improve your work environment, at least in the short term. You might have really connected with a couple of ideas, while disagreeing with others. That's what makes us people, not machines.

Similarly, my purpose in *The End of Office Politics as Usual* has been to get you thinking about what you'd like to change in your own work environment and how to turn your vision into a reality. If you are working in a political environment, I hope this book has validated your belief that there is a better way of doing business. And if you now have the confidence and courage in your beliefs to do something about it, we've both won.

Notes

1   Robert S. Kaplan and David P. Norton, *The Balanced Scorecard* (Cambridge: Harvard Business School Press, 1996).

Epilogue

I sincerely hope that I have made a difference for you and your work life. While you might not be able to implement all of the ideas expressed in this book and certainly not on your own, your simply raising the issues surrounding office politics, especially those pertaining to organizational performance, might get people listening. That's enough of a start.

They say a problem once recognized is half solved. If your coworkers are able to do a little soul-searching and recognize that office politics are creating performance issues, you'll find a way to address them. Hopefully you've found helpful ideas about how to do just that in this book.

If you have a story about office politics and the enemy within, I'd love to hear it. You can reach me at lserven@msn.com. Remember, we're all in this together, and we learn more from other people's experiences. I've enjoyed sharing with you what I've learned so far and look forward, with your help, to making a difference.

Resources

Argyris, Christopher. "Skilled Incompetence." *Harvard Business Review* (September–October 1986): 77.

Bick, Julie. *All I Ever Need to Know in Business I Learned at Microsoft.* New York: Pocket Books, 1997.

Bloomfield, Harold, M.D. *Healing Anxiety With Herbs.* New York: Harper-Collins, 1998.

Buffett, Warren. Berkshire Hathaway, Inc., *1989 Annual Report.* Omaha, Neb.

Burke, Ronald J. "Issues and Implications for Health Care Delivery Systems: A Canadian Perspective." In *Work Stress: Health Care Systems in the Workplace,* edited by James Quick, Rabi Bhagat, James Dalton, and Jonathan Quick. New York: Praeger, 1987.

Case, John. *Open-Book Management.* New York: HarperBusiness, 1996.

Cowley, Michael, and Ellen Domb. *Beyond Strategic Vision.* Boston: Butterworth-Heinemann, 1997.

Deming, W. Edwards. *Out of the Crisis.* Cambridge, Mass.: MIT Center for Advanced Engineering Study, 1982.

Doorley, Thomas L., and John M. Donovan. *Value Creating Growth.* San Francisco: Jossey-Bass, 1999.

Freil, John, and Linda Freil. *An Adult Child's Guide to What Normal Is.* Deerfield Beach, Fla.: Health Communications, 1990.

Gardell, Bertil. "Efficiency and Health Hazards in Mechanized Work." In *Work Stress: Health Care Systems in the Workplace*, edited by James Quick, Rabi Bhagat, James Dalton, and Jonathan Quick. New York: Praeger, 1987.

Geneen, Harold, and Alvin Moscow. *Managing*. Garden City, N.Y.: Doubleday, 1984.

Havens, Leston. *A Safe Place*. Cambridge, Mass.: Harvard University Press, 1989.

Health, Education, and Welfare Department, *Work in America: Report of a Special Task Force to the U.S. Department of Health, Education, and Welfare*. Cambridge, Mass.: MIT Press, 1973.

Helgesen, Sally. *The Web of Inclusion*. New York: Doubleday, 1995.

Kaplan, Robert S. and David P. Norton, *The Balanced Scorecard* Cambridge: Harvard Business School Press, 1996.

Lebow, Rob, and William Simon. *Lasting Change: The Shared Values That Make a Company Great*. New York: Van Nostrand Reinhold, 1997.

Lichtenberg, Ronna. *Work Would Be Great if It Weren't for the People*. New York: Hyperion Press, 1998.

Marshall, Edward. *Building Trust at the Speed of Change: The Power of the Relationship-Based Organization*. New York: AMACOM, 1999.

McTaggart, James; Peter Kontes, and Michael Mankins. *The Value Imperative*. New York: The Free Press, 1994.

New Economy Incentives Survey. Stamford, Connecticut: The Buttonwood Group, 2000.

Quick, James. "Preventing Stress Intervention: A Challenging Area for Researchers." In *Work Stress: Health Care Systems in the Workplace*, edited by James Quick, Rabi Bhagat, James Dalton, and Jonathan Quick. New York: Praeger, 1987.

Quick, James, Rabi Bhagat, James Dalton, and Jonathan Quick, eds. *Work Stress: Health Care Systems in the Workplace*. New York: Praeger, 1987.

Reinhold, Barbara Bailey. *Toxic Work: How to Overcome Stress, Overload, and Burnout and Revitalize Your Career.* New York: Dutton Books, 1996.

Ryan, Kathleen D. *Driving Fear out of the Workplace.* San Francisco: Jossey-Bass, 1998.

Serven, Lawrence. *Value Planning: The New Approach to Building Value Every Day.* New York: John Wiley & Sons, 1998.

———. *A Survey on Corporate Initiatives.* Stamford, CT: The Buttonwood Group, 1999.

Simmons, Annette. *Territorial Games: Understanding and Ending Turf Wars at Work.* New York: AMACOM, 1997.

"21st Century Planning," *CFO Magazine,* (Feb. 1998), 30.

Van Slyke, Erik J. *Listening to Conflict: Finding Constructive Solutions to Workplace Disputes.* New York: AMACOM, 1999.

Weisbord, Marvin. *Productive Workplaces: Organizing for Dignity, Meaning, and Community.* San Francisco: Jossey-Bass, 1987.

Index

About the Author

Lawrence Serven is a founder and principal of The Buttonwood Group, a research and consulting firm specializing in organizational effectiveness, leadership development, and performance management. His firm helps companies implement high-performance, collaborative workplaces. Among other honors, *CFO Magazine* has recognized Lawrence as a leading authority on business planning.

His best-selling book, *Value Planning: The New Approach to Building Value Every Day* (John Wiley & Sons, 1998) describes a battle-tested approach to driving shareholder value by integrating long-range and operational planning with performance management, reporting, and executive compensation.

This former Fortune 500 executive has led engagements for clients in the entertainment, financial services, consumer goods, direct mail, manufacturing, insurance, retail, and pharmaceutical industries, as well as for public sector organizations.

Lawrence has chaired leading management conferences across the United States and Canada, and has been a featured speaker at *CFO Magazine*'s CFO Rising, the New York Society of Securities Analysts, the American Institute of Certified Public Accountants, the National Investor Relations Institute, the Georgia State CFO Roundtable, and other signature events.

Lawrence is also the author of several management articles that have appeared in *The Harvard Management Update, Investor Relations, Financial Executive, The Journal of Accountancy, Financial Executive, Chief Information Officer,* and *Executive Excellence.* Lawrence's work has been profiled in *CFO Magazine, The NYSSA News, The Exchange Magazine, The Financial Accounting Report,* and others.

Lawrence is a *summa cum laude* graduate of Boston College with a BA in Economics. He earned an MBA from the Fuqua School of Business at Duke University.

He can be reached at LServen@msn.com.